CHRISTIAN HISTORY: BIOGRAPHIES OF FAITH

- Weekly Lesson Schedule
- Student Worksheets
- Quizzes & Tests
- Answer Key

First printing: September 2014

Copyright © 2014 by Master Books®. All rights reserved. No part of this book may be used or reproduced in any manner whatsoever without written permission of the publisher, except in the case of brief quotations in articles and reviews. For information write:

Master Books®, P.O. Box 726, Green Forest, AR 72638

Master Books® is a division of the New Leaf Publishing Group, Inc.

ISBN: 978-0-89051-850-2

Unless otherwise noted, Scripture quotations are from the New King James Version of the Bible.

Printed in the United States of America

Please visit our website for other great titles:

www.masterbooks.net

For information regarding author interviews,

please contact the publicity department at (870) 438-5288

Since 1975, Master Books has been providing educational resources based on a biblical worldview to students of all ages. At the heart of these resources is our firm belief in a literal six-day creation, a young earth, the global Flood as revealed in Genesis 1–11, and other vital evidence to help build a critical foundation of scriptural authority for everyone. By equipping students with biblical truths and their key connection to the world of science and history, it is our hope they will be able to defend their faith in a skeptical, fallen world.

If the foundations are destroyed, what can the righteous do?
Psalm 11:3; NKJV

As the largest publisher of creation science materials in the world, Master Books is honored to partner with our authors and educators, including:

Ken Ham of Answers in Genesis

Dr. John Morris and Dr. Jason Lisle of the Institute for Creation Research

Dr. Donald DeYoung and Michael Oard of the Creation Research Society

Dr. James Stobaugh, John Hudson Tiner, Rick and Marilyn Boyer, Dr. Tom DeRosa, Todd Friel, Israel Wayne, and so many more!

Whether a pre-school learner or a scholar seeking an advanced degree, we offer a wonderful selection of award-winning resources for all ages and educational levels.

*But sanctify the Lord God in your hearts, and always be ready
to give a defense to everyone who asks you a reason for the hope
that is in you, with meekness and fear.*
1 Peter 3:15; NKJV

Permission to Copy

Permission is granted for copies of reproducible pages from this text to be made for use within your own homeschooling family activities or for small classrooms of ten or fewer students. Material may not be posted online, distributed digitally, or made available as a download. Permission for any other use of the material must be requested prior to use by email to the publisher at nlp@newleafpress.net.

Lessons for a 36-week course!

Overview: This *Christian History: Biographies of Faith PLP* contains materials for use with *Life of John Newton*, *Life of Washington*, *Life of Andrew Jackson*, *Life of John Knox*, and *Life of Luther*. Materials are organized by each book in the following sections:

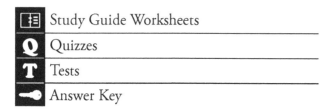

- Study Guide Worksheets
- Quizzes
- Tests
- Answer Key

Features: Each suggested weekly schedule has five easy-to-manage lessons that combine reading, worksheets, and vocabulary-building opportunities. Worksheets, quizzes, and tests are perforated and three-hole punched — materials are easy to tear out, hand out, grade, and store. Adjust the schedule and materials needed to best work within your educational program.

Workflow: Students will read the pages in their book and then complete each section of the PLP. They should be encouraged to complete as many of the worksheets as possible as well. Quizzes and tests are given at regular intervals with space to record each grade.

Lesson Scheduling: Space is given for assignment dates. There is flexibility in scheduling. For example, the parent may opt for a M–W schedule rather than a M, W, F schedule. Each week listed has five days. Adapt the days to your school schedule. As the student completes each assignment, he/she should put an "X" in the box.

🕐	Approximately 30 to 45 minutes per lesson, five days a week	*Life of Washington*: Anna C. Reed, niece of a signer of the Declaration of Independence.
🗝	Includes answer keys for worksheets, quizzes, and tests	*Life of Andrew Jackson*: John S. Jenkins, American author who wrote historical works and biographies.
📋	Worksheets for each reading portion	*Life of Luther*: Barnas Sears served in leadership areas of education and pastoral ministry.
↻	Quizzes and tests are included to help reinforce learning and provide assessment opportunities	*Life of John Knox*: The book of this reformer was originally published by the ASSU in 1833.
📄	Designed for grades 7 to 9 in a one-year course to earn 1 history credit	*Life of John Newton*: The book of this Christian author and minister was originally published by the ASSU in 1831.

Contents

Suggested Daily Schedule 7

Worksheets
    Life of Washington Worksheets..13
    Life of Andrew Jackson Worksheets...31
    Life of Luther Worksheets..61
    Life of John Knox Worksheets...95
    Life of John Newton Worksheets..103

Quizzes and Tests
    Life of Washington Quizzes..115
    Life of Andrew Jackson Quizzes...123
    Life of Luther Quizzes..131
    Life of John Knox Quizzes...141
    Life of John Newton Quizzes...143
    Life of Andrew Jackson Test..147
    Life of Luther Test...149
    Life of Knox and Newton Test..151

Answer Key
    Life of Washington Worksheets..155
    Life of Andrew Jackson Worksheets...160
    Life of Luther Worksheets..167
    Life of John Knox Worksheets...175
    Life of John Newton Worksheets..177
    Life of Washington Quizzes..179
    Life of Andrew Jackson Quizzes...181
    Life of Luther Quizzes..183
    Life of John Knox Quizzes...186
    Life of John Newton Quiz..187
    Life of Washington Test Quizzes..188
    Life of Andrew Jackson Test..188
    Life of Luther Test...188
    Life of Knox and *Newton* Test..189

Introduction

An exceptional study on faith and leadership that focuses on the US presidents Washington and Jackson, as well as the Christian reformers Knox, Newton, and Luther. Students will discover their influences, struggles, and accomplishments, and take away lessons on the lives of these great leaders. Are great men simply born great or do they make a choice in their life to be something more? Study the lives of these Christian men to discover how they were transformed by their faith, moral values, and pure courage.
In this unique course, students will go beyond historical footnotes to really see what has been revealed about their hearts, their fears, and their vision for changing the world as they knew it. An inspiring study designed to encourage students to lead!

Explanation of Activities

Vocabulary: Students should define each of the words. If they know the word, they should define it in their own words. If they do not know the word, they should use a dictionary to search for its meaning. Many of the words chosen are presented in a secondary or archaic usage. Students should define the word in the context of its usage in the book.

Short Answer: Students should answer these questions in complete sentences. Most of them can be answered in three sentences or less.

Long Answer: These questions are essentially the same as short-answer questions but are broader in scope and require a longer answer, though not long enough to be considered an essay. Students should answer these questions in paragraph form, and they will often take more than a single paragraph to completely answer.

Bonus Activities to Explore More: Each chapter will contain one or more optional bonus activities. Most of these activities require further research and may also require materials beyond the books and the PLP. Select the activities that are best suited for your individual needs.

Due to time constraints with this course, some small sections of the books will not be covered by the PLP. It is recommended that these pages be read if it will fit within your schedule, but they will not be required material.

Special Projects

It is recommended that the student complete a four-page research paper each semester of the course. In semester one, the student should choose a president other than Washington or Jackson and research his Christian faith and how it affected his actions. (John Quincy Adams, Abraham Lincoln, and James Garfield would all make interesting subjects.) Similarly, in the second semester students should choose a reformer other than Knox or Luther and research his Christian faith and how it affected his actions. (John Calvin, Huldrych Zwingli, John Wycliffe, and Jan Hus would all make interesting subjects.)

A Note about Grading

Because this course is focused on conceptual themes such as character and leadership, the best way to assess learning is through broad, open-ended questions. Thus, assigning grades can be more difficult. Please feel free to assign partial credit to the short- and long-answer questions. Students should always be expected to use proper grammatical practices.

First Semester Suggested Daily Schedule

Date	Day	Assignment	Due Date	✓	Grade
		First Semester-First Quarter			
Week 1	Day 1	Read Pages 19-30 • *Life of Washington* • (LOW)			
	Day 2	Read Pages 31-45 • (LOW)			
	Day 3	1732–1762 **Ch1: Worksheet 1** • Pages 15-16 • Lesson Planner • (LP)			
	Day 4	Read Pages 45-55 • (LOW)			
	Day 5	Read Pages 56-69 • (LOW)			
Week 2	Day 6	1763–1776 **Ch2: Worksheet 1** • Pages 17-18 • (LP)			
	Day 7	Read Pages 69-85 • (LOW)			
	Day 8	Read Pages 86-100 • (LOW)			
	Day 9	1776–1777 **Ch3: Worksheet 1** • Pages 19-20 • (LP)			
	Day 10	Study Day for Quiz 1			
Week 3	Day 11	**Quiz 1 - Life of Washington (Ch 1-3)** • Pages 115-116 • (LP)			
	Day 12	Read Pages 108-120 • (LOW)			
	Day 13	Read Pages 121-133 • (LOW)			
	Day 14	1777–1780-Words to Know **Ch5: Worksheet 1** • Page 21 • (LP)			
	Day 15	1777–1780-Short Answers/Activities **Ch5: Worksheet 1** • Pages 21-22 • (LP)			
Week 4	Day 16	Read Pages 141-153 • (LOW)			
	Day 17	Read Pages 157-159, 170-181 • (LOW)			
	Day 18	1780, 1780-1781 **Ch6-7: Worksheet 1** • Pages 23-24 • (LP)			
	Day 19	Study Day for Quiz 2			
	Day 20	**Quiz 2 - Life of Washington (Ch 5-7)** • Pages 117-118 • (LP)			
Week 5	Day 21	Read Pages 182-200 • (LOW)			
	Day 22	Read Pages 201-211 • (LOW)			
	Day 23	1781-1787 **Ch8-9: Worksheet 1** • Pages 25-26 • (LP)			
	Day 24	Read Pages 212-227 • (LOW)			
	Day 25	Read Pages 228-242 • (LOW)			
Week 6	Day 26	1787--1796 **Ch10-11: Worksheet 1** • Pages 27-28 • (LP)			
	Day 27	Study Day for Quiz 3			
	Day 28	**Quiz 3 - Life of Washington (Ch 8-11)** • Pages 119-120 • (LP)			
	Day 29	Read Pages 242-259• (LOW)			
	Day 30	Read Pages 265-277 • (LOW)			

Date	Day	Assignment	Due Date	✓	Grade
Week 7	Day 31	1796-1799, Conclusion **Ch12-Conclusion: Worksheet 1** • Pages 29-30 • (LP)			
	Day 32	Study Day for Quiz 4			
	Day 33	**Quiz 4 - Life of Washington (Ch 12-Con.)** • Pgs 121-122 • (LP)			
	Day 34	Study Day for Unit 1 Test			
	Day 35	**Unit 1 Test - Life of Washington** • Pages 145-146 • (LP)			
Week 8	Day 36	Read Pages 12-18 • *Life of Andrew Jackson* • (LOAJ)			
	Day 37	Read Pages 19-23 • (LOAJ)			
	Day 38	1767 **Ch1: Worksheet 1** • Pages 33-34 • Lesson Planner • (LP)			
	Day 39	Read Pages 24-30 • (LOAJ)			
	Day 40	Read Pages 31-36 • (LOAJ)			
Week 9	Day 41	1789 **Ch2: Worksheet 1** • Pages 35-36 • (LP)			
	Day 42	Read Pages 37-43 • (LOAJ)			
	Day 43	Read Pages 44-49 • (LOAJ)			
	Day 44	1804 **Ch3: Worksheet 1** • Pages 37-38 • (LP)			
	Day 45	Study Day for Quiz 5			
		First Semester-Second Quarter			
Week 1	Day 46	**Quiz 5 - Life of Andrew Jackson (Ch 1-3)** • Pgs 123-124 • (LP)			
	Day 47	Read Pages 50-56 • (LOAJ)			
	Day 48	Read Pages 57-62 • (LOAJ)			
	Day 49	1813-Words to Know **Ch4: Worksheet 1** • Page 39 • (LP)			
	Day 50	1813-Short Answer/Activities **Ch4: Worksheet 1** • Pages 39-40 • (LP)			
Week 2	Day 51	Read Pages 63-72 • (LOAJ)			
	Day 52	Read Pages 73-81 • (LOAJ)			
	Day 53	1813 **Ch5: Worksheet 1** • Pages 41-42 • (LP)			
	Day 54	Read Pages 82-87 • (LOAJ)			
	Day 55	Read Pages 88-93 • (LOAJ)			
Week 3	Day 56	1814 **Ch6: Worksheet 1** • Pages 43-44 • (LP)			
	Day 57	Study Day for Quiz 6			
	Day 58	**Quiz 6 - Life of Andrew Jackson (Ch 4-6.)** • Pgs 125-126 • (LP)			
	Day 59	Read Pages 94-102 • (LOAJ)			
	Day 60	Read Pages 103-111 • (LOAJ)			

Date	Day	Assignment	Due Date	✓	Grade
Week 4	Day 61	1814 **Ch7: Worksheet 1** • Pages 45-46 • (LP)			
	Day 62	Read Pages 113-123 • (LOAJ)			
	Day 63	Read Pages 124-136 • (LOAJ)			
	Day 64	1814-Words to Know **Ch8: Worksheet 1** • Page 47 • (LP)			
	Day 65	1814-Short Answer/Activities **Ch8: Worksheet 1** • Pages 47-48 • (LP)			
Week 5	Day 66	Read Pages 138-146 • (LOAJ)			
	Day 67	Read Pages 147-154 • (LOAJ)			
	Day 68	1815 **Ch9: Worksheet 1** • Pages 49-50 • (LP)			
	Day 69	Study Day for Quiz 7			
	Day 70	**Quiz 7 Life of Andrew Jackson (Ch 7-9.) • Pgs 127-128** • (LP)			
Week 6	Day 71	Read Pages 155-162 • (LOAJ)			
	Day 72	Read Pages 163-169 • (LOAJ)			
	Day 73	1815-Words to Know **Ch10: Worksheet 1** • Page 51 • (LP)			
	Day 74	1815 **Ch10: Worksheet 1** • Pages 51-52 • (LP)			
	Day 75	Read Pages 170-176 • (LOAJ)			
Week 7	Day 76	Read Pages 177-182 • (LOAJ)			
	Day 77	1821-Words to Know **Ch11: Worksheet 1** • Page 53 • (LP)			
	Day 78	1821-Short Answer/Activities **Ch11: Worksheet 1** • Pages 53-54 • (LP)			
	Day 79	Read Pages 184-189 • (LOAJ)			
	Day 80	Read Pages 190-193 • (LOAJ)			
Week 8	Day 81	1837-Words to Know **Ch12: Worksheet 1** • Page 55 • (LP)			
	Day 82	1837-Short Answer/Activities **Ch12: Worksheet 1** • Pages 55-56 • (LP)			
	Day 83	Study Day for Quiz 8			
	Day 84	**Quiz 8 - Life of Andrew Jackson (Ch 10-12) • Pgs 129-130** • (LP)			
	Day 85	Read selection from appendix (See Ch 13 - WS1 for details)			
Week 9	Day 86	Appendices **Ch13: Worksheet 1** • Pages 57-58 • (LP)			
	Day 87	Read selection from appendix (See Ch 13 - WS2 for details)			
	Day 88	Appendices **Ch13: Worksheet 2** • Pages 59-60 • (LP)			
	Day 89	Study Day for Unit 2 Test			
	Day 90	**Unit 2 Test - Life of Andrew Jackson** • Pages 147-148 • (LP)			
		Mid-Term Grade			

Second Semester Suggested Daily Schedule

Date	Day	Assignment	Due Date	✓	Grade
		Second Semester-Third Quarter			
Week 1	Day 91	Read Pages 15-25 • *Life of Luther* • (LOL)			
	Day 92	Read Pages 34-47 • *Life of Luther* • (LOL)			
	Day 93	Birth to age 14 **Part 1, Ch1: Worksheet 1** • Pages 63-64 • (LP)			
	Day 94	Read Pages 48-58 • (LOL)			
	Day 95	Read Pages 59-69 • (LOL)			
Week 2	Day 96	1497 to 1505 **Part 1, Ch2: Worksheet 1** • Pages 65-66 • (LP)			
	Day 97	Read Pages 70-80 • (LOL)			
	Day 98	Read Pages 81-90 • (LOL)			
	Day 99	1505 to 1508 **Part 1, Ch3: Worksheet 1** • Pages 67-68 • (LP)			
	Day 100	Study Day for Quiz 9			
Week 3	Day 101	**Quiz 9 - Life of Luther (Part 1, Ch 1-3)** • Pages 131-132 • (LP)			
	Day 102	Read Pages 91-105 • (LOL)			
	Day 103	Read Pages 106-119 • (LOL)			
	Day 104	1505 to 1508-Words to Know **Part 1, Ch3: Worksheet 2** • Page 69 • (LP)			
	Day 105	1505 to 1508-Short Answer/Activities **Part 1, Ch3: Worksheet 2** • Pages 69-70 • (LP)			
Week 4	Day 106	Read Pages 120-121, 125-129 • (LOL)			
	Day 107	Read Pages 132-137, 148-159 • (LOL)			
	Day 108	1508 to 1517 **Part 1, Ch4: Worksheet 1** • Pages 71-72 • (LP)			
	Day 109	Read Pages 159-170 • (LOL)			
	Day 110	Read Pages 171-181 • (LOL)			
Week 5	Day 111	1508 to 1517 **Part 1, Ch4: Worksheet 2** • Pages 73-74 • (LP)			
	Day 112	Study Day for Quiz 10			
	Day 113	**Quiz 10 - Life of Luther (Part 1, Ch 3-4)** • Pages 133-134 • (LP)			
	Day 114	Read Pages 183-194 • (LOL)			
	Day 115	Read Pages 195-201 • (LOL)			
Week 6	Day 116	1517 to 1518 **Part 2, Ch1: Worksheet 1** • Pages 75-76 • (LP)			
	Day 117	Read Pages 201-211 • (LOL)			
	Day 118	Read Pages 212-222 • (LOL)			
	Day 119	1517 to 1518-Words to Know **Part 2, Ch1: Worksheet 2** • Page 77 • (LP)			
	Day 120	1517 to 1518-Short Answer/Activities **Part 2, Ch1: Worksheet 2** • Pages 77-78 • (LP)			

Date	Day	Assignment	Due Date	✓	Grade
Week 7	Day 121	Read Pages 222-230 • (LOL)			
	Day 122	Read Pages 231-240 • (LOL)			
	Day 123	1517 to 1518 **Part 2, Ch1: Worksheet 3** • Pages 79-80 • (LP)			
	Day 124	Read Pages 240-251 • (LOL)			
	Day 125	Read Pages 260-269 • (LOL)			
Week 8	Day 126	1517 to 1518 **Part 2, Ch1: Worksheet 4** • Pages 81-82 • (LP)			
	Day 127	Study Day for Quiz 11			
	Day 128	**Quiz 11 - Life of Luther (Part 2, Ch 1)** • Pages 135-136 • (LP)			
	Day 129	Read Pages 270-275 • (LOL)			
	Day 130	Read Pages 287-301 • (LOL)			
Week 9	Day 131	Leipsic Disputation **Part 2, Ch2: Worksheet 1** • Pages 83-84 • (LP)			
	Day 132	Read Pages 302-314 • (LOL)			
	Day 133	Read Pages 315-326 • (LOL)			
	Day 134	Luther and Diet of Worms-Words to Know **Part 2, Ch3: Worksheet 1** • Page 85 • (LP)			
	Day 135	Luther and Diet of Worms-Short Answer/Activities **Part 2, Ch3: Worksheet 1** • Pages 85-86 • (LP)			

Second Semester-Fourth Quarter

Date	Day	Assignment	Due Date	✓	Grade
Week 1	Day 136	Read Pages 327-337 • (LOL)			
	Day 137	Read Pages 338-347 • (LOL)			
	Day 138	1521 to 1525 **Part 2, Ch4: Worksheet 1** • Pages 87-88 • (LP)			
	Day 139	Study Day for Quiz 12			
	Day 140	**Quiz 12 - Life of Luther (Part 2, Ch 2-4)** • Pages 137-138 • (LP)			
Week 2	Day 141	Read Pages 347-360 • (LOL)			
	Day 142	Read Pages 361-374 • (LOL)			
	Day 143	1521 to 1525 **Part 2, Ch4: Worksheet 2** • Pages 89-90 • (LP)			
	Day 144	Read Pages 375-386 • (LOL)			
	Day 145	Read Pages 387-399 • (LOL)			
Week 3	Day 146	Luther's Marriage and Domestic Life **Part 2, Ch5: Worksheet 1** • Pages 91-92 • (LP)			
	Day 147	Read Pages 399-407 • (LOL)			
	Day 148	Read Pages 408-416 • (LOL)			
	Day 149	Luther's Marriage and Domestic Life **Part 2, Ch5: Worksheet 2** • Pages 93-94 • (LP)			
	Day 150	Study Day for Quiz 13			

Date	Day	Assignment	Due Date	✓	Grade
Week 4	Day 151	**Quiz 13 - Life of Luther (Part 2, Ch 4-5)** • Pages 139-140 • (LP)			
	Day 152	Study Day for Unit 3 Test			
	Day 153	**Unit 3 Test - Life of Luther** • Pages 149-150 • (LP)			
	Day 154	Read Pages 9-28 • *Life of John Knox* • (LOJK)			
	Day 155	Read Pages 29-45 • (LOJK)			
Week 5	Day 156	Introduction to Mary of Guise **Intro-Ch4: Worksheet 1** • Pages 97-98 • (LP)			
	Day 157	Read Pages 45-68 • (LOJK)			
	Day 158	Read Pages 69-88 • (LOJK)			
	Day 159	A solemn covenant to Wicked joy **Ch5-8: Worksheet 1** • Pages 99-100 • (LP)			
	Day 160	Read Pages 89-110 • (LOJK)			
Week 6	Day 161	Read Pages 111-140 • (LOJK)			
	Day 162	The assembly to End **Ch9-13: Worksheet 1** • Pages 101-102 • (LP)			
	Day 163	Study Day for Quiz 14			
	Day 164	**Quiz 14 - Life of John Knox (Inro-13)** • Pages 141-142 • (LP)			
	Day 165	Read Pages 5-20 • *Life of John Newton* • (LOJK)			
Week 7	Day 166	Read Pages 21-45 • (LOJK)			
	Day 167	Biography to From Cape de Verd **Ch1-Ch3: Worksheet 1** • Pages 105-106 • (LP)			
	Day 168	Read Pages 45-65 • (LOJK)			
	Day 169	Read Pages 66-85 • (LOJK)			
	Day 170	Newton's situation to After his marriage **Ch4-Ch6: Worksheet 1** • Pages 107-108 • (LP)			
Week 8	Day 171	Read Pages 85-100 • (LOJK)			
	Day 172	Read Pages 101-115 • (LOJK)			
	Day 173	After a short stay **Ch7: Worksheet 1** • Pages 109-110 • (LP)			
	Day 174	Read Pages 115-130 • (LOJK)			
	Day 175	Read Pages 131-144 • (LOJK)			
Week 9	Day 176	After a short stay to End **Ch7-Review: Worksheet 2** • Pages 111-112 • (LP)			
	Day 177	Study Day for Quiz 15			
	Day 178	**Quiz 15 - Life of John Newton (Ch 1-7)** • Pages 143-144 • (LP)			
	Day 179	Study Day for Unit 4 Test			
	Day 180	**Unit 4 Test - Life of Knox and Newton** • Pages 151-152 • (LP)			
		Final Grade			

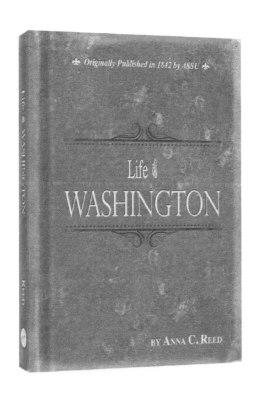

Biographical Worksheets

for Use with

Life of Washington

| | *Life of Washington* | 1732–1762 Pages 19–45 | Day 3 | Chapter 1 Worksheet 1 | Name |

Words to Know – Define each term in the context it is presented in the book.

indulgence

midshipmen

ascertain

anecdote

filial

aide-de-camp

Short Answer

1. Describe the importance of Washington's relationship with his mother.

2. Explain the circumstances that led the British into a war with the French in 1754.

3. "The resolution with which Washington had performed the duty entrusted to him, and the judgment he had shown in his conduct towards the Indians, gained the favourable opinion of the people of the province, as well as that of the governor, and he was appointed lieutenant-colonel of the regiment. . . ." What does the quote above tell us about developing a good reputation?

4. How did the way Washington handled the surrender at Ft. Necessity win him the confidence of his countrymen?

5. Why did Washington resign his commission in 1754? Do you agree with his decision to do so? Why or why not?

6. General Braddock's actions at the Monongahela River have become known in history as "Braddock's Blunder." What did he do to earn this title?

7. What prompted the field physician to say, "Nothing but the superintending care of Providence could have saved him from the fate all around him"?

8. Pages 44–45 share a powerful anecdote about the generosity and sincerity of Washington. Read Matthew 6:1–4 and explain its relevance to that anecdote.

9. What does it say about Washington's character that "those who were nearest to him, and knew him best, loved him most"?

10. What valuable lessons did Washington learn in his first 27 years that you think benefitted him later on in life when he was president of the United States?

Activities

1. The author shares the famous story of young Washington chopping down his father's cherry tree, but admits that she is unable to ascertain on what authority it is related. Using outside resources, research what others have said about the veracity of this anecdote and decide if it is indeed a reliable piece of information.

| *Life of Washington* | 1763–1776 Pages 45–69 | Day 6 | Chapter 2 Worksheet 1 | Name

Words to Know – Define each term in the context it is presented in the book.

resolute

magistrate

unanimity

unostentatiously

huzzahing

heretofore

prudent

approbation

pecuniary

Short Answer

1. In response to Parliament's actions toward Massachusetts, several colonial legislatures set aside a day for fasting, prayer, and worship to plead for God's help, support, and direction. If America faced a similar circumstance today, do you think our states would have the same response? Why or why not?

2. What is implied about Washington's character that he was notable and recognizable because he was "the gentleman who kneels down" when Congress goes to prayer?

3. How did Washington get the nickname "The Virginia Patriot"?

4. What reasons are given for why Washington was unanimously chosen as commander-in-chief of the Continental Army?

5. Describe the response of Washington to his appointment as commander-in-chief.

6. This chapter explains that Washington had a very strong temper from his youngest days and had to work hard to keep it under control. Read the following verses and summarize their significance with regard to controlling anger:

    a. Ephesians 4:26

    b. James 1:19–20

    c. Ecclesiastes 7:9

    d. Proverbs 22:24–25

Activities

1. From the period of 1763 to 1776, create a timeline of significant events leading up to the American Declaration of Independence. Annotate the timeline to provide context for each event listed.

2. This chapter notes the "dignity" of Washington's manners. To get a good idea about what is meant by that statement, read pages 260–265. These pages contain a few of Washington's *Rules of Civility & Decent Behaviour In Company and Conversation*. This was a list of 110 rules for decent social behavior that Washington had transcribed by the time he was 16. If you want, read the entire list, which can be found online. Create a list of ten of your own rules of decent behavior, and make a concerted effort to live by them.

| Life of Washington | 1776–1777 Pages 69–100 | Day 9 | Chapter 3 Worksheet 1 | Name

Words to Know – Define each term in the context it is presented in the book.

veneration

melancholy

sundry

candour (candor)

imputation

presumption

mortification

imprudently

Tories

Short Answer

1. What significance would you ascribe to the fact that the members of the Second Continental Congress chose to add references to God into the final draft of the Declaration of Independence?

2. Why did Washington refuse to negotiate with General Howe? What does this incident reveal about Washington's character?

3. In the first year of the war, the Americans saw little success. How did this affect morale, and how did Washington deal with this issue?

First Semester/First Quarter // 19

4. Using Washington's own words (found in chapter 3), describe his plan for fighting the early days of the war.

5. Describe the way Providence allowed Washington to remove his troops from Long Island.

6. Describe the miraculous way Washington was able to capture 1,000 men at Trenton with only the loss of two of his own men.

7. What revolutionary action did Washington take to protect his army from smallpox?

8. "I shall never forget what I felt when I saw him brave all the danger of the field . . . he is surely in heaven's peculiar care."

    Based on what you have read so far (ch. 1–3), describe three incidents that could be used as evidence to support this assertion about Washington's divine protection.

Activities

1. Do some research on inoculation in the 1700s and then write a short paper (one page or less) describing the procedure and what it must have been like that winter in Morristown when Washington's soldiers were inoculated.

2. Compare Thomas Jefferson's rough draft to the final version of the Declaration of Independence. What items were added and what items were deleted? Why do you think those changes were made?

3. Find a copy of Emanuel Leutze's famous painting, *Washington Crossing the Delaware*. Look closely for any historical inaccuracies. Research the particulars of this work and you'll find out about these "errors."

| *Life of Washington* | 1776–1777 Pages 108-133 | Day 14 & 15 | Chapter 5 Worksheet 1 | Name |

Words to Know – Define each term in the context it is presented in the book.

repine

inclinations

miscreant

fidelity

impious

abominable

imprecations

wanton

Short Answers

1. Describe Washington's response to the rumor that he was considering resigning during that difficult winter at Valley Forge.

2. Describe Washington's dining habits at Valley Forge. What do they reveal about his character?

3. What did Joseph Reed mean when he told the British officers that he was "not worth buying; but, such as he was, the king of England was not rich enough to do it"?

4. Contrary to popular opinion today, Washington did face oppositions from some of his own people. Several people sent unsigned letters to Congress accusing Washington of impropriety. Describe how Washington responded to this opposition.

5. The text describes three eyewitness accounts of Washington's devotion to prayer. Describe each of these accounts.

6. Read Matthew 6:6. How did Washington's prayer life reflect this passage of Scripture?

7. How did Washington respond to the dispute between General Sullivan and the French admiral D'Estaing?

8. What did Washington mean when he wrote, "The hand of Providence is so conspicuous in all this, that he must be worse than an infidel that lacks faith, and more than wicked, that has not gratitude to acknowledge his obligations"?

9. Describe the order issued by Washington to his troops on July 29, 1779.

10. Where you surprised to learn of this order? Again, what does this order say about the character of Washington?

Activities

1. This chapter briefly mentions the role of women in the Revolutionary War. Research this topic and write a brief (one page or less) description of the important role women played in the war effort. Cite specific examples (i.e., Molly Pitcher).

| Life of Washington | 1780-1781 Pages 141-181 | Day 18 | Chapters 6-7 Worksheet 1 | Name |

Words to Know – Define each term in the context it is presented in the book.

dissipation

depraved

sloop

deluded

mutiny

impropriety

conflagration

Short Answer

1. Pages 141–153 recount the story of how Benedict Arnold became the nation's most famous traitor. In the space below, briefly recount what led to this infamy.

2. How do you think Washington felt about having one of his most-decorated generals do such a thing? How would you have reacted?

3. Page 152 talks about "chance" and "accidents." Based on what you've learned from this text, does it appear to you that the ultimate success of the Americans was due to just "chance," or do you think it was the Providence of God? Explain.

4. Pages 157–159 share an anecdote about General Marion and the American spirit during the war. What did the British officer in the story learn about Marion and the Americans?

5. Men under General Wayne attempted to march on Congress to demand provisions for the feeble Continental Army. How did Washington handle this? How does this incident show the wisdom of Washington?

6. With regard to Lafayette, how did General Cornwallis fail to benefit from the truth of 1 Timothy 4:12?

7. Recount the story of what happened when Washington's home was facing the threat of being burned by the British. What was Washington's response and what does that reveal about his character?

8. Why did Washington refuse to aid his native state, Virginia?

9. "Every one, who with piety notices the providences of God, can know that our best blessings are often hid beneath our disappointments, as sweet flowers are concealed in bitter buds."

    Explain the meaning of this statement. Have you found this to be true? Give an example from your life.

10. Describe the crucial role that Mr. Robert Morris played in the war effort.

Activities

1. Several American generals are discussed in these two chapters (6–7). Choose one of them (besides Washington, of course) and do some further research on them. Present this research in the form of a short paper (one page or less), in a computer-generated presentation, or orally.

| Life of Washington | 1781-1787 Pages 182-211 | Day 23 | Chapters 8-9 Worksheet 1 | Name |

Words to Know – Define each term in the context it is presented in the book.

eminence

posterity

deportment

felicity

ardently

procured

diffidence

rectitude

sanguine

august body

venerable

Short Answer

1. As Cornwallis and his men marched out of Yorktown in defeat, how did Washington address his men?

2. Describe Washington's visit to his mother in 1781.

3. After the war concluded, soldiers again clamored for their pay from the bankrupt Congress. How did Washington deal with this incident, what was the result, and what does it reveal about his character?

4. A few new recruits marched to Philadelphia and demanded that Congress pay them within twenty minutes. Describe Washington's reaction when he heard this news.

5. Describe the response of Washington to his nephew Bushrod, who had failed to complete a promise made to his uncle.

6. Explain the manner in which Washington kept his financial account with the government.

7. After retiring from military service, where did Washington put his efforts?

8. Chapter 9 closes with a comparison of the American and French Revolutions. What is the point made by the author?

9. According to the text, how should you view your freedom?

Activities

1. Research the provisions of the Treaty of Paris, 1783. What did the United States receive as a result of this negotiation?

2. Do a keyword search for the word "freedom" in the Bible using a Bible concordance or online search. Write a paragraph that summarizes a biblical worldview on that subject.

| Life of Washington | 1787-1789, 1789-1796 Pages 212-242 | Day 26 | Chapters 10-11 Worksheet 1 | Name |

Words to Know – Define each term in the context it is presented in the book.

dissolution

concourse

tranquility

homage

conspicuous

meritorious

unremitted

privateer

insolent

Short Answer

1. Summarize Benjamin Franklin's address to the members of the Constitutional Convention.

2. Describe Washington's response to his election as president.

3. Analyze the following quote from Washington: "My past actions, rather than my present declarations, must be the pledge of my future conduct." Would you say that politicians today practice the truth of this statement?

4. Describe Washington's views on punctuality.

5. What was the main source of trouble during Washington's second term in office, what was his strategy for dealing with it, and why did he choose that strategy?

6. In 1794, the Whiskey Rebellion erupted in western Pennsylvania. What was it about, and what was Washington's response?

7. The author strongly warns the reader of the dangers of "strong drink." What reasons are given for this? Find two verses of Scripture that support these assertions.

8. Both chapters 10 and 11 share stories of encounters between Washington and ordinary citizens. In light of these anecdotes, what could be said about the feelings of the American people toward him and his relationship with them?

Activities

1. Read Washington's farewell address. In a paragraph or two, summarize his instructions and warnings to the people.

2. This chapter mentions the role of Benjamin Franklin at the Constitutional Convention. Franklin's faith has been the subject of much historical discussion and debate. However, we do know for sure that Franklin had a very cordial and interesting relationship with George Whitfield, the greatest preacher of the era. Do a little research into this relationship.

3. This book was published in 1842 during the height of the Second Great Awakening. The author's views on the topic of intoxicating liquors are no doubt affected by the temperance movement that accompanied this American religious revival. Research some of the major individuals, organizations, and events of the temperance movement.

| *Life of Washington* | 1787-1789, 1789-1796 Pages 242-277 | Day 31 | Ch12-Conclusion Worksheet 1 | Name |

Words to Know – Define each term in the context it is presented in the book.

idleness

dispositions

indigent

frank

trifling

benefactor

inculcated

abhorrence

proffered

solicitude

Short Answer

1. Describe Washington's daily routine after he returned home from the presidency.

2. According to pages 246–247, what role did Washington think religion should play in politics?

3. Give a specific example of how Washington cared for the poor.

4. Washington was called on once again to lead the American military in 1798. What led to this?

5. Briefly recount the events culminating in Washington's death.

6. Many contemporary scholars suggest that Washington was not a Christian, or at best was only a deist. Based on the evidence given in this book (particularly in the conclusion), refute that conclusion.

7. The author closes with, "Was he not worthy of your imitation?" Giving specific examples, answer this question.

Activities

1. Plan a visit to Mt. Vernon! Nothing could help you understand better what it was like for Washington to ride through his farm, examining it on a daily basis. The grounds are still kept in impeccable condition and the estate is a national treasure.

2. The text mentions the portraits of Washington painted by Charles Wilson Peale. Compare these portraits to ones done by John Trumbull and Gilbert Stuart. What are the similarities and differences? Which do you think is the most accurate reflection of the true character? Why?

3. The account of Washington's death includes many terms that are no longer in popular usage and procedures that reflected the limited medical knowledge of the time. Research the meaning of these items and see if you can ascertain the actual cause of Washington's death. Terms to look for include: ague, bleed (as in, to "bleed" a patient), sal volatile, blister of flies, calomel, and tarter emetic.

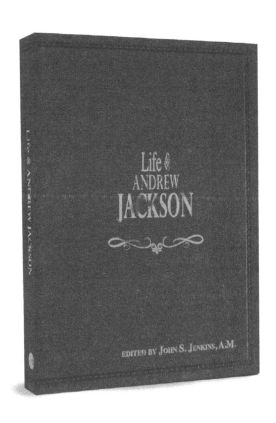

Biographical Worksheets

for Use with

Life of Andrew Jackson

| Life of Andrew Jackson | 1767 Pages 12-23 | Day 38 | Chapter 1 Worksheet 1 | Name |

Words to Know – Define each term in the context it is presented in the book.

incipient

surplice

habiliments

imbrued

sallying

dragoons

execration

assuage

redoubt

patrimony

desultory

Short Answer

1. Read the preface of the book. What is the purpose of the book, according to the author?

2. What can you assume about the political climate of the time (1850), based on the author's statements in the preface?

3. What do you think the author meant by this statement: "Whatever may be the views entertained in regard to his merits as a warrior, or his abilities as a statesman, his conduct in both capacities was such as must necessarily command attention"?

4. Like Washington, Jackson's father died while Jackson was only a child. How do you think that affected his upbringing?

5. How did Jackson's Scotch-Irish background affect his view of the American crusade for independence (particularly his view of the British government)?

6. Jackson was forced to take up arms for his country when he was only a young teen. How do you think this affected his development as a person?

7. Describe the incident that left a scar on Jackson's left hand.

8. By the end of the war, all of Jackson's family had died. What happened next in his life?

9. Read Luke 15:11–32. How does Jackson's young adulthood compare to this story? How is it different?

10. At the age of 21, Jackson left his home to travel to Tennessee and start the next chapter of his life. What events and lessons of his first 21 years do you think shaped him most?

Activities

1. The book mentions that Jackson staked his horse against a sum of money in a game of "rattle and snap." See if you can find out how this game was played.

2. Jackson was a very unlikely candidate for future president by his 21st year. He was ill-educated, left without family, and hardened from the death and destruction of the war. Do some research to compare his childhood to the childhood of other presidents. Was there any other president who was less likely, based on childhood, to assume that role?

3. Map Activity: This chapter has many town names and battle sites. Print or draw a blank map of North and South Carolina. Label all of these places mentioned in chapter 1. Annotate the map with information to make it usable for someone reading this text.

| Life of Andrew Jackson | 1767 Pages 24-36 | Day 41 | Chapter 2 Worksheet 1 | Name |

Words to Know – Define each term in the context it is presented in the book.

cataract

circuitous

churlishness

bivouac

writs

provocation

depredation

appellation

morose

affability

expostulate

posse comitatus

dirk

remonstrate

inimical

Questions

1. As a budding lawyer on the western frontier, Jackson made 22 trips into the dangerous backwoods country of Tennessee. What do we learn about the character of Jackson during this time?

2. In order, list the various public positions held by Jackson between 1790 and 1804.

3. When Jackson first moved to Tennessee, it was full of men who prided themselves on fighting and were always ready to start one. How did Jackson deal with these kinds of characters?

4. Where did Jackson earn the title "Sharp Knife"?

5. Jackson was "devotedly fond" of his wife, Rachel. Recount the story of how he found and married her.

6. What kind of reputation did Jackson develop as a judge?

7. "General Jackson was distinguished throughout his whole life for a remarkable fidelity to his friends." While we would generally consider this to be a good quality in a person, how could this fidelity to friends lead to problems?

8. Jackson always distrusted his abilities as a judge, and even resigned his post after four years. Why do you think this was the case?

Activities

1. If you read the text closely, you see that Jackson's marriage happened before Rachel's divorce from her first husband had been finalized, leading some of Jackson's critics to label her a bigamist. Research the details of this incident and how it plagued Jackson for the rest of his public life.

2. The Alien and Sedition Acts of 1798 are two of the most controversial pieces of legislation in all of American history. Jackson was not present to vote for the Sedition Act and voted against the Alien Act. Research these laws to find out why they were passed, what their provisions were, and why Jackson would have been opposed.

36 // First Semester/First Quarter

| Life of Andrew Jackson | 1804 Pages 37-49 | Day 45 | Chapter 3 Worksheet 1 | Name |

Words to Know – Define each term in the context it is presented in the book.

officious

promptitude

reconnoitre

privation

presage

censure

caucus

calamitous

torpor

Short Answer

1. How did Jackson end up in his infamous duel with Charles Dickinson? What does this event reveal about Jackson's character?

2. What did Jackson do once he found out that his partner in business had racked up more debt than he could afford?

3. What reason did Jackson give when refusing to procure a passport while traveling into Mississippi?

4. How do you think Jackson would view the security measures that our country uses today?

5. What does it say about Jackson that although he was shot in a duel with Thomas H. Benton, they became strong political allies later in life?

6. According to the text, why was Jackson quick to volunteer for the war against Great Britain?

7. Why did Jackson refuse to abide by the order handed down to him by the Secretary of War on January 5, 1813?

8. Jackson is notable for fostering a fierce loyalty from those who served him. Based on what you have learned so far, why do you think that was the case?

Activities

1. This chapter briefly discusses the outbreak of the War of 1812, but gives few details regarding the causes of the war. One detail mentioned is the Embargo Act of 1807. Research this act as well as the broader causes of the War of 1812 and write a one-page explanation.

2. "The reputation of General Wilkinson, who had been appointed to supplant Jackson, was also tarnished, by his unfortunate operations in Canada, during the campaign of 1814." Research this incident to find out what the author meant by this statement.

3. Thomas Hart Benton is a name that was connected to Jackson throughout most of the men's adult lives. Research this other "voice of the west" and his relationship with Jackson.

4. It may seem like a strange way to settle disputes, but at that point in history it was fairly commonplace to duel — particularly in the south. In order to better comprehend dueling, research the Code Duello. This code of conduct related to duels will help you better understand the framework that Jackson was working with when a duel was challenged.

| Life of Andrew Jackson | 1813 Pages 50-62 | Day 49 & 50 | Chapter 4 Worksheet 1 | Name |

Words to Know – Define each term in the context it is presented in the book.

imperious

forbearance

ardor

bane

accoutrements

lassitude

consternation

trepidation

discomfiture

indemnified

Short Answer

1. When the Native Americans are the aggressors in battle, they are presented as savages, but when the white Americans are the aggressors, they are presented as valiant and noble. Why do you think that is the case, and do you feel that is a fair assessment? Why or why not?

2. Describe the attention given to discipline by General Jackson. Why was he so rigid?

3. As Jackson marched his men out, he was continuously plagued by what difficulty?

4. This chapter contains two addresses Jackson gave to his men. Summarize the contents of these speeches.

5. What happened to the orphaned Indian boy at the Battle of Tallushatchee? Does this reveal anything significant about the character of Andrew Jackson?

6. What is the name of Jackson's residence?

Activities

1. The Indian chief Tecumseh is presented as an antagonist in this chapter. He was, however, a brilliant leader and managed to do something that the Native Americans rarely did effectively — organize across tribal boundaries. Do some research on Tecumseh and find out what qualities made him a successful leader.

2. Plan a visit to the Hermitage! Located just outside of Nashville, Tennessee, this home has quite a history. If an actual visit isn't possible, try a virtual visit online.

| Life of Andrew Jackson | 1813 Pages 63-81 | Day 53 | Chapter 5 Worksheet 1 | Name |

Words to Know – Define each term in the context it is presented in the book.

amicable

rivulet

offal

repast

tripe

wo-begone

chagrined

sumptuous

auspiciously

satiety

expatiated

Short Answer

1. At the conclusion of the Battle of Talladega, how were provisions acquired?

2. Review page 69. How could the charity of Jackson be compared to Washington?

3. What was the meal that Jackson shared with a hungry soldier? What was the result of this encounter?

4. Most of chapter 5 deals with the difficulties Jackson faced in obtaining food for his men. As a result of this issue, the men attempted mutiny several times. Using several examples from the chapter, explain how Jackson was able to keep his men from leaving.

5. How would you describe the leadership displayed by Jackson during this trying time? What characteristics were admirable? Where there any characteristics that were not so admirable? Would you have handled it differently?

Activities

1. Map Activity: Print or draw a map of the southeastern United States. Plot all of the places mentioned in this chapter on the map.

2. There have been many mutinies in history that did not end as favorably as this one. Research one of these others to examine what can happen when soldiers are discontented. (For example, you could choose the notorious mutiny on the *Bounty*, or perhaps the *Meermin* slave ship mutiny.)

| Life of Andrew Jackson | 1814 Pages 82-93 | Day 56 | Chapter 6 Worksheet 1 | Name |

Words to Know – Define each term in the context it is presented in the book.

intrepidity

defile

grapeshot

incantation

disinterred

flambeaux

husbandry

prevaricated

impunity

Short Answer

1. What happened to the young Indian wounded in the battle near Tohopeka?

2. Colonel Milton asked Captain Gordon what sort of man General Jackson was. What was Captain Gordon's answer? How did Milton respond to Gordon's answer?

3. How would you answer the question, "What sort of man was General Jackson?"

4. Summarize the contents of the proclamation issued by Edward Nicholls from the fort at Pensacola.

5. Based on what you've read, do you think Jackson's assault of Pensacola was justified? Give reasons to support your answer.

Activities

1. Jackson's attack on Pensacola was the subject of a congressional investigation. Find out why he was investigated and what the investigation concluded about Jackson's actions.

2. Page 89 tells us that General Harrison resigned his post in the Army in 1814. That is William Henry Harrison, future president of the United States. Do a one-page summary of the life and accomplishments of William Henry Harrison.

| *Life of Andrew Jackson* | 1814 Pages 94-111 | Day 61 | Chapter 7 Worksheet 1 | Name |

Words to Know – Define each term in the context it is presented in the book.

formidable

feint

evinced

concerted

yeomanry

sally

temerity

impervious

alacrity

Short Answer

1. What is martial law, and why did Jackson put New Orleans under it?

2. How did Jackson respond to the women of New Orleans who were shrieking in fear? What was the result?

3. Most of this chapter deals with the offensive maneuver of the American forces on December 23, 1814. To summarize, explain how the American force, though vastly outnumbered, was so successful that night.

4. Although the Americans had very decided advantages, at the end of the night Jackson chose not to pursue and conquer the enemy. How did he come to this difficult conclusion?

5. How badly were Jackson's men outnumbered by the British forces?

Activities

1. The author has spoken very fondly of General Coffee, one of Jackson's subordinates, several times in the text. Research General John Coffee to find out why Jackson trusted him so deeply and thought favorably of him.

2. Review the history of the city of New Orleans. Unlike most of the east coast of the United States, this area had a complex history of changing hands through various treaties. Why would Jackson take the sorts of precautions he did in a place like 1814 New Orleans?

| Life of Andrew Jackson | 1814 Pages 113-136 | Day 64 & 65 | Chapter 8 Worksheet 1 | Name |

Words to Know – Define each term in the context it is presented in the book.

sagacity

judicious

exigencies

overweening

conjecture

embrasures

videttes

scruple

assiduity

palliate

nefarious

ambuscade

Short Answer

1. According to the text, what were the distinguishing traits in the character of General Jackson as a military commander?

2. "When to expect an attack, he could not tell; preparation and readiness to meet, were for him to determine upon; all else was for the enemy." How could this statement also be true of our spiritual lives?

3. What did Jackson NOT do between December 23 and December 27? Why not?

4. What strategic order did Jackson give to keep the British troops from attacking a hundred yards below his current position?

5. What did Jackson mean when he said, "the surest defence, and one which seldom failed of success, was a rampart of high-minded and brave men"?

6. Mr. Shields and Dr. Murrell were detained by a British admiral. How were they able to mislead the admiral into believing that there were 20,000 American troops, when there were actually only 2,000?

7. What were Jackson's plans if the British had actually overtaken his fortifications and forced an American retreat? Why was this his plan?

8. What was Jackson's response to the Frenchman who was upset about his property being seized for the war effort?

Activities

1. Analyze the paintings based on the Battle of New Orleans by Jean Hyacinthe de Laclotte and Edward Percy Moran.

2. The next chapter will spend a great deal of time explaining the penultimate Battle of New Orleans. It would be wise to download a map of the battlefield to use as a reference while you read.

| Life of Andrew Jackson | 1815 Pages 138-154 | Day 68 | Chapter 9 Worksheet 1 | Name |

Words to Know – Define each term in the context it is presented in the book.

incessant

precipitately

abatement

impetuousity

galled

licentious

cupidity

debase

enmity

dastardly

gibbet

glacis

Short Answer

1. Why were the long-awaited reinforcements from Kentucky not as helpful as had been hoped? How did Jackson wisely deal with this problem?

2. Why did the main force of the British army attack the position held by General Carroll?

3. What was the author implying when he stated that the General "seldom slept: he was always at his post, performing the duties of both general and soldier"?

4. On pages 147–148, a comparison is made between the ethics of the American soldiers and the ethics of the British soldiers. Summarize this section of text.

5. Most of the chapter deals with the strategic actions of the battle. Based on what you've read, why were the Americans able to defeat a much larger and better trained British army?

6. The author states, "It was impossible for men to serve under such a leader as Jackson, without becoming imbued with the same dauntless courage which he always exhibited." Why do you think Jackson was able to do this?

7. Provide the description of Jackson's character as a general that is found at the top of page 152.

8. How does the British account of the battle differ from that told in this book?

Activities

1. Listen to and analyze the famous song, "The Battle of New Orleans," written by Jimmy Driftwood and made popular by Johnny Horton in 1959. How historically accurate is the song?

2. Likewise, listen to "The Hunters of Kentucky," a Jackson presidential campaign tune. Why was this an effective piece of campaign propaganda?

| *Life of Andrew Jackson* | 1815 Pages 155-169 | Day 73 & 74 | Chapter 10 Worksheet 1 | Name |

Words to Know – Define each term in the context it is presented in the book.

encomium

rapine

fortitude

pomp

incendiaries

parleying

writ of habeas corpus

extricate

Short Answer

1. How did New Orleans respond to Jackson's successful defense of the city?

2. Why did Jackson have Judge Hall arrested?

3. What is significant about the date on which the Treaty of Ghent was signed?

4. What happened after Jackson received a $1,000 fine from Judge Hall?

5. Why is Jackson often referred to as Old Hickory?

6. What important job was Jackson awarded after he left New Orleans and fought in the Seminole Campaign?

7. "Although the measures he adopted appeared harsh, the American people were ready to approve his conduct, when it was ascertained that it originated in a desire to carry out his own noble sentiment, that 'the great can protect themselves, but the poor and humble require the arm and shield of the law' " (page 168). Do you agree with this statement? Why or why not?

Activities

1. Analyze the Treaty of Ghent. What did the United States really achieve as a result of this war?

2. Jackson was fined $1,000 by Judge Hall. Using an inflation calculator (easily found online or as a cell phone application) determine how much money that sum would be equivalent to today. What does this tell us about Jackson?

3. A treaty was signed on February 22, 1819. Research the key provisions of this treaty.

52 // First Semester/Second Quarter

| *Life of Andrew Jackson* | 1821 Pages 170-182 | Day 77 & 78 | Chapter 11 Worksheet 1 | Name |

Words to Know – Define each term in the context it is presented in the book.

plenopotientiary

partisans

bereavment

irreparable

averred

aloof

parlance

temerity

asperity

chivalric

Short Answer

1. Why was Jackson in poor health by 1821?

2. The election of 1824 has become known in history as the "Corrupt Bargain." Though this text doesn't explicitly use that terminology, explain why Jackson supporters came up with this label.

3. What attacks were made on Jackson as he ran in the 1828 presidential election?

4. How was Jackson affected by the death of his wife?

5. Page 176 refers to Jackson as the "rock of Gibraltar." What is the statement in reference to, and what is the implication it makes?

6. The text says that Jackson's "opinions could not be changed, and the line of conduct he had marked out was fixed and unalterable." Would you consider this a good or bad quality for a leader to have? Explain.

7. What do the results of the 1832 election show about Jackson?

8. How did Jackson respond to Mr. Randolph's attempted assault?

9. In 1835, under Jackson, the public debt was completely liquidated. What has happened to the public debt since then? Where does it stand now?

Activities

1. The nomination process for selecting candidates for the presidential election is much different today than in 1824. Research the history of the nomination process to get a better understanding of how there were four candidates in the 1824 election.

2. The book vaguely mentions the resignation of Mr. Eaton, secretary of war, because of "family relations." This was actually a reference to Mrs. Eaton, who was not well received by the other wives of cabinet members. Research to find out more about the "Eaton Affair," since it undermined Jackson's effectiveness for his entire first term as president.

3. The 1832 election saw the introduction of our nation's first third party, the Anti-Masons. Research this group to find out what other "firsts" they hold, and what their political issues were.

4. Do some research to find out why Mr. Randolph wanted to assault President Jackson. This was not the only attempt on the life of President Jackson. Find out the details of the other one.

| Life of Andrew Jackson | 1837 Pages 184-193 | Day 81 & 82 | Chapter 12 Worksheet 1 | Name |

Words to Know – Define each term in the context it is presented in the book.

dropsy

swooned

rancorous

bedew

intuitive

celerity

groveling

Short Answer

1. What did Congress do for Jackson in the 1844–45 session?

2. Summarize Jackson's religious statements made on his deathbed.

3. How would you reconcile Jackson's Christian confession with the many acts of violence he committed throughout his lifetime?

4. Summarize the remarks of Reverdy Johnson, a senator in Congress from the state of Maryland, and a political opponent of General Jackson, upon hearing of Jackson's death.

5. Pages 191–193 make the case that Jackson was no ordinary man, and in many respects could be considered one of the most remarkable men who ever lived. Summarize the evidence given for this argument.

6. Make a T-chart below. On the right side, list the positive qualities you see in Jackson. On the left, list the negative qualities.

Activities

1. Explore the deathbed statements of other United States presidents. One of the more curious incidents involves the deaths of John Adams and Thomas Jefferson, who both died on July 4, 1826.

| *Life of Andrew Jackson* | Appendicies Pages 194-222, 304-341 | Day 86 | Chapter 13 Worksheet 1 | Name

Write a Summary

Chapter 13 serves as an appendix of twelve documents related to the life and times of Andrew Jackson. For this week's assignment, choose one of the following to read. After reading, write a summary in the space below. Use the table of contents to find the page numbers.

- Bancroft's Eulogy, page 194
- Jackson's Inaugural Address, page 219
- Jackson's Sixth Annual Message, page 304

| *Life of Andrew Jackson* | Appendicies Pages 348-370, 379-395 | Day 88 | Chapter 13 Worksheet 2 | Name |

Write a Summary

Chapter 13 serves as an appendix of twelve documents related to the life and times of Andrew Jackson. For this week's assignment, choose one of the following to read. After reading, write a summary in the space below. Use the table of contents to find the page numbers.

- Jackson's Farewell Address, page 348
- Dr. Bethune's Discourse, page 379

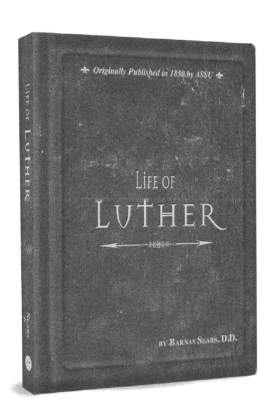

Biographical Worksheets

for Use with

Life of Luther

| Life of Luther | Birth to age 14 Pages 15-25, 34-47 | Day 93 | Part 1 Chapter 1 Worksheet 1 | Name |

Words to Know – Define each term in the context it is presented in the book.

edifice

declivity

penury

obstinacy

gamboling

turbid

credulous

knaves

cogitations

drollery

sottish

Short Answer

1. Describe the character of Luther's father. How did this affect Luther's efforts later in life when he committed himself to the work of reforming the church?

2. What effects did Luther's mother have on her son?

3. Page 23 gives one of the main reasons for the writing of this text. What was that reason?

4. Luther was subject to harsh discipline both by his parents and his earliest educators. What effect do you think this had on his development?

5. How does the author describe the state of the Catholic Church at the time of Luther's education?

6. How did the German church differ from the Italian church at this time?

7. Some regard Luther as the sort of person who brought about change as a result of a "well-planned scheme." This author disagrees. How is Luther described instead (page 38)?

8. How was Luther raised to view Christ?

9. How did Luther's socio-economic background and geographic location benefit his efforts to reform the Church?

Activities

1. Find a German map and locate the places where young Luther was born, raised, and educated.

2. The book describes the Catholic Church as a "Pelagian system." Find out who Pelagius was and what his teachings embodied.

Life of Luther | 1497 to 1505 Pages 48-69 | Day 96 | Part 1 Chapter 2 Worksheet 1 | Name

Words to Know – Define each term in the context it is presented in the book.

mendicant

scapularies

cowl

trifling

pensive

indelibly

chagrin

capacious

prolix

cloister

propound

Short Answer

1. How did Luther provide for himself while in his early schools?

2. Describe the painting Luther saw while at the Franciscan school. Why did this have such an effect on him?

3. What impact did Madam Cotta have on the young Luther?

4. How were Luther's years at the University of Erfurt significant to his intellectual development?

5. Summarize the prophetic word an old priest gave to Luther while he was very ill at Madgeburg.

6. Describe Luther's first encounter with a Bible.

7. How was Luther able to go into adulthood without ever seeing a Bible? What does this tell you about the nature of the Church at this time in history?

Activities

1. Luther spent some time in a Franciscan school. Do some research to find out about Franciscans and Catholic orders in general.

2. Explore how access to the Bible was restricted during the Middle Ages. How was change brought about?

| *Life of Luther* | 1505 to 1508 Pages 70-90 | Day 99 | Part 1 Chapter 3 Worksheet 1 | Name

Words to Know – Define each term in the context it is presented in the book.

propagate

novitiate

languor

antiphonies

genuflection

collation

acquiescence

vitiated

mote

demure

colloquy

Short Answer

1. Why were Luther's three years at Erfurt so significant to his later reform efforts?

2. What two ideas did Luther first began to explore at Erfurt — ideas that would later be the backbone of the Reformation?

3. Generally speaking, why did Luther consider becoming a monk?

4. Specifically, what incident led him to make a vow to become a monk?

5. Analyze the biblical debate between Luther's father and the friars over Luther's decision to join the cloister. Who do you think was right?

6. Though one could easily see Luther's years in the convent as a waste, the author argues that God ordered that Luther should become a monk. Why?

7. Describe what life was like for Luther in his first year as a novice monk.

8. What was the problem Luther had with the practice of confession?

9. Describe the monastic process of biblical interpretation as outlined in this chapter.

10. Luther paints a very negative picture of the monastic life. What led him to this position?

Activities

1. This chapter explores Luther's association with the Augustinian order. How does it differ from the Franciscan order?

| *Life of Luther* | 1505 to 1508 Pages 91-119 | Day 104 & 105 | Part 1 Chapter 3 Worksheet 2 | Name |

Words to Know – Define each term in the context it is presented in the book.

efficacious

mien

benighted

disquisition

execrable

ablution

lucre

parricide

raillery

adduce

cumbrous

Short Answer

1. In spite of an unfulfilling first year, Luther would not leave the cloister. Why not?

2. Why is Luther's relationship with Staupitz described as "the most important acquaintance which Luther ever formed"?

3. Why was Luther very concerned about becoming a priest?

4. Later in life, Luther became very critical of the mass. Why?

5. Pages 114–115 lay out basic differences between the Catholic and Protestant faiths. Summarize the contents of this section.

6. How did the phrase "the righteousness of God" take on new meaning for Luther?

Activities

1. John von Staupitz is a crucial character in the story of Martin Luther. Although chapter 3 gives some biographical information about him, research him a bit further.

| *Life of Luther* | 1508 to 1517 Pages 120-159 | Day 108 | Part 1 Chapter 4 Worksheet 1 | Name

Words to Know – Define each term in the context it is presented in the book.

refectory

luminous

exculpate

vehement

Short Answer

1. What was peculiar about Luther's initial appointment to the University of Wittenberg?

2. What was unique about the administrative structure of the university, which would greatly favor the Reformation?

3. Describe the social and religious atmosphere of the university upon Luther's arrival.

4. How much was Luther paid during his first semester of lecturing on Aristotle?

5. In 1509, Luther was called upon to begin preaching. He was extremely reluctant. How did he overcome this? What spiritual lessons could be learned from this incident?

6. Why did the oath that Luther took upon receiving his doctor of divinity become important for his later defense of the Reformation?

7. Why was Luther's study of Greek and Hebrew crucial to his spiritual formation?

8. What do Luther's letters from 1515 reveal about his development as a person?

Activities

1. The text alludes on several occasions to the problems of the Latin Vulgate. Find out why many Protestants take issue with the Vulgate.

| *Life of Luther* | 1508 to 1517 Pages 159-181 | Day 111 | Part 1 Chapter 4 Worksheet 2 | Name

Words to Know – Define each term in the context it is presented in the book.

disputations

maledictions

pernicious

ignominiously

decorous

erudite

obstreperous

Short Answer

1. Why is 1516 an important year when studying the biography of Martin Luther?

2. Why did Luther come to hate Aristotle?

3. Luther was made vicar of the order in Saxony and Thuringia in place of Staupitz for about a year and a half, or from April 1516 to about November of 1517. What was different about Luther's reaction to this appointment, compared to previous appointments? What can we infer from this difference?

4. Much of this section is given to quotations of letters written by Luther. The purpose is to present a picture of how Luther had developed by the time the Reformation began. With that in mind, summarize the social, intellectual, and theological changes that had taken hold of Luther by early 1517.

Activities

1. The author mentions "Bunyan's pilgrim" as a comparison to the conversion of Luther. If you have never read *Pilgrim's Progress*, obtain a copy and read this classic work!

| *Life of Luther* | 1517 to 1518 Pages 183-201 | Day 116 | Part 2 Chapter 1 Worksheet 1 | Name

Words to Know – Define each term in the context it is presented in the book.

contrariety

nominally

plenary

sepulchre

legate

itinerating

degeneracy

transient

Short Answer

1. Page 184 contrasts two systems related to the removal of sin. Summarize the difference between the two on this issue.

2. Why did Luther refer to the priest as having "assumed a false position in the church"?

3. What three successful acts were required for absolution of sin?

4. What were Luther's primary concerns with this process of absolution?

5. Describe the role that indulgences had come to play in the church by Luther's time.

6. Summarize the character and actions of Tetzel that led him to be a major target of Luther's complaints.

7. Name three key individuals who were arguing many of the same points as Luther, but several years before.

Activities

1. This chapter mentions another Catholic order — the Dominicans. Find out what makes this order unique.

2. It might be worthwhile to read a Catholic assessment of Tetzel. Do the Catholics condone his actions? Do they even agree with the assessment of his character made in this text?

| | *Life of Luther* | 1517 to 1518 Pages 201-222 | Day 119 & 120 | Part 2 Chapter 1 Worksheet 2 | Name |

Words to Know – Define each term in the context it is presented in the book.

decalogue

servile

abstruse

confuted

impugn

superlatively

supercilious

inveighed

fulminate

odium

corpulent

magnanimity

Short Answer

1. Rather than buy indulgences, how did Luther suggest that Christians should spend their money? Why?

2. How did Luther deal with members of his own congregation who presented him with their indulgences?

3. Why did Luther resort to posting his 95 theses on October 31?

4. What evidence exists to suggest that Luther wasn't really trying to instigate a public rebellion with his 95 theses? Why did he publish a simpler version of his arguments?

5. Summarize the initial public reaction to the theses.

Activities

1. To add a greater context to this reading, read a copy of the 95 theses (which are easily obtained online). Which ones do you find the most controversial?

| *Life of Luther* | 1517 to 1518 Pages 222-240 | Day 123 | Part 2 Chapter 1 Worksheet 3 | Name |

Words to Know – Define each term in the context it is presented in the book.

parsimonious

puerile

decretals

dogmas

prefatory

enigmatically

requital

promulgated

sordid

Short Answer

1. Summarize the contents of Luther's letter to Staupitz on May 30, 1518. Why is it of "great historical value"?

2. On the same day, Luther wrote a letter to Leo X. Again, summarize its contents and explain its significant historical value.

3. What was Luther's initial reaction to his summons to appear at Rome for trial?

4. Who is described as Luther's "truest and ablest associate" in the struggle for truth? Why did he come to the university?

5. At this point in Luther's life (mid-1518), how would you describe Luther's relation with the Catholic Church? Was he still loyal, or had he already made up his mind to break away?

Activities

1. Research the background of Melancthon, a key reformer and asset to Luther.

| *Life of Luther* | 1517 to 1518 Pages 240-269 | Day 126 | Part 2 Chapter 1 Worksheet 4 | Name

Words to Know – Define each term in the context it is presented in the book.

paternoster

unapt

nuncio

peradventure

hellebore

potentates

plenitude

Short Answer

1. Page 241 contains this quote from Luther: "Still, I sincerely regard ecclesiastical authority." Considering the context, do you think he was being completely sincere? Explain.

2. What two errors did the papal legate in Augsburg ask Luther to confess and drop? What was Luther's response?

3. After Staupitz's intervention, Luther was asked to only recant his article on indulgences. According to Staupitz, what did this reveal about Rome?

4. What three demands did Luther agree to during his interview with Miltitz in January 1519?

5. The author states, "Luther was not perfect, was not always consistent, nor always right either in his opinions or in his feelings. Far from it." Provide evidence to support this statement.

Activities

1. Read a Catholic assessment of the life of Luther. Compare and contrast the version told here. What are the differences?

| | Life of Luther | Leipsic Disputation Pages 270-301 | Day 131 | Part 2 Chapter 2 Worksheet 1 | Name |

Words to Know – Define each term in the context it is presented in the book.

disengenuous

sycophancy

contumely

suborned

perfidious

chasuble

garrulity

gesticulation

polemic

adroitness

perdition

spurious

Short Answer

1. What three men took part in the public debate in Leipsic in the summer of 1519?

2. Why did Luther participate in the debate if he had promised Miltitz that he would remain silent?

3. "In respect to a rupture with Rome, there is an apparent inconsistency in Luther at this time." What does the author mean by this statement, and what is the explanation given for this apparent inconsistency?

4. Read Romans 13:1–7. Do you think Luther's actions accurately reflected the truth of this passage? Explain.

5. What were the consequences of the great debate at Leipsic?

6. After the debate, Luther was very busy with scholarly writing. What work of his is considered the "chief work" in which the fundamental principles of the Reformation are laid down?

Activities

1. Luther refers to the papacy as the "power of Nimrod." Find out what Luther meant by this by reading Genesis 10, and researching the significance of Nimrod.

2. By 1520, Luther had become convinced that the pope was the antichrist. Research this concept. Find out what others have said about this assumption.

| *Life of Luther* | Luther and Diet of Worms Pages 302-326 | Day 134 & 135 | Part 2 Chapter 3 Worksheet 1 | Name |

Words to Know – Define each term in the context it is presented in the book.

escutcheon

iota

bespeaking

preconcerted

exchequer

cavalcade

Short Answer

1. Why was the political climate of Germany conducive to the Reformation?

2. Why was the Roman party at the Diet of Worms strongly opposed to bringing Luther in for examination?

3. What did Luther expect from the Diet of Worms? What does it say about his character that he went anyway?

4. What two questions were posed to Luther by the Diet?

5. What was Luther's initial response to the questions? What was the response of the Diet?

6. How did Luther finally answer the Diet the next day? Carefully explain his logic and reasoning.

7. He was accused of evading the question and asked to give a direct answer. Recount this final answer.

8. What admirable qualities do you see in the way Luther handled this interrogation?

Activities

1. Page 307 mentions the Italian reformer and martyr Savonarola. Find out who he was and what happened to him. Is his story comparable to Luther's?

2. The book mentions Luther's memorable prayer made during the hours between his first and second appearance before the Diet, but it doesn't provide you with the text. Look it up and analyze it. How do you think Luther felt in that moment?

3. Many scholars today claim that the line, "Here I stand, and cannot do otherwise," was not in fact stated by Luther at the Diet. Explore this claim, and decide whether you think he did say it, or did not.

| *Life of Luther* | 1521 to 1525 Pages 327-347 | Day 138 | Part 2 Chapter 4 Worksheet 1 | Name

Words to Know – Define each term in the context it is presented in the book.

costiveness

derision

auricular

prelate

aspersion

jocosely

Short Answer

1. Luther spent ten months in hiding at Wartburg. Why was this time favorable to his character?

2. How did Luther's view on religious liberty evolve during this period and the years thereafter?

3. What was Luther's reaction to the renewed selling of indulgences by Albert, Archbishop of Mainz?

4. Why did Spalatin and Melancthon intervene into this conflict between Luther and Albert? How does this incident show the importance of accountability in Christian relationships?

5. What new problems and questions arose from the beginning of the Reformation and threatened to halt its momentum?

6. What was the main issue dividing Luther and Carlstadt?

7. Why did Luther finally come out of hiding and once again join in the battle raging throughout the country, even though his life was clearly still in some degree of danger?

Activities

1. This chapter explores the problems created by the Reformation. In particular, it mentions the Anabaptists and Zwinglians. Research each of these and figure out what the major points of difference were.

| Life of Luther | 1521 to 1525 Pages 347-374 | Day 143 | Part 2 Chapter 4 Worksheet 2 | Name

Words to Know – Define each term in the context it is presented in the book.

harangued

ribaldry

courtiers

expostulation

dissimulation

inveterate

grotesque

Short Answer

1. Upon arriving back at Wittenberg, what was Luther's primary criticism of his followers there?

2. Luther felt that many people in the movement were trying to move to quickly toward change. Give a couple of examples of this, and explain Luther's reasoning for moving more slowly.

3. What circumstances allowed Luther to carry on his work undisturbed by political forces?

4. "Luther never loved those who taught differently than himself. . . . This was a fault in his character." Examine this statement (found on page 367) and explain why you think Luther was this way. What might have been different had Luther been more beneficent toward his opposition?

5. Summarize the major points of debate between Carlstadt and Luther in the early 1520s.

6. Explain the difference between transubstantiation and consubstantiation. (This will require an outside source.)

7. What was the major mistake both Luther and Carlstadt made in the course of this dispute?

8. "He was a better theologian than politician." What was the circumstance that led the author to make this criticism of Luther?

Activities

1. Research Erasmus to find out why he was held in such high esteem and why Luther was so concerned about his opinion.

2. To fully understand the situation of Germany in the 1520s, one needs to gain context by exploring the political climate of the time. Do this by researching the German Peasants' War.

3. Find out why Luther had concerns about the Book of James. Do you think his concerns were justifiable?

Life of Luther | *Luther's Marriage Pages 375-399* | Day 146 | Part 2 Chapter 5 Worksheet 1 | Name

Words to Know – Define each term in the context it is presented in the book.

fetters

tattled

amanuensis

conjugal

circumlocution

avarice

Short Answer

1. Describe how Luther arranged for nine nuns to be broken out of their convent and released to freedom.

2. Why did Luther hesitate to take a wife, even though he now had the freedom of conscience to do so?

Second Semester/Fourth Quarter // 91

3. Yet, not long afterward, Luther was married to Catherine von Bora. The marriage was done privately, and only afterward were people apprised of it. Why did Luther not tell people (even some of his closest associates) that he was getting married?

4. How would you characterize the marriage of Martin and Catherine?

5. Describe the way Luther handled money.

Activities

1. For a better look at much of the personal information regarding the life of Luther, read the final chapter (6), which includes many excerpts from personal letters.
2. Luther was prone to fits of melancholy or depression. This text only briefly deals with this issue, but it is a very interesting part of Luther's character. Using outside sources, find out how Luther dealt with this issue in his life.

| Life of Luther | Luther's Marriage Pages 399-416 | Day 149 | Part 2 Chapter 5 Worksheet 2 | Name |

Words to Know – Define each term in the context it is presented in the book.

castigate

vivacity

amorous

Short Answer

1. Describe the qualities that made Luther an excellent orator and preacher.

2. Why was Luther such a strong supporter of public education? How does this figure prominently into the Reformation?

3. According to Luther, what role should parents play in the education of their children?

4. Summarize Luther's feelings about the role of music in a Christian's life.

5. Based on everything you have learned about the life of Luther, what qualities made him a likely candidate to bring about the Reformation? What qualities made him an unlikely candidate?

Activities

1. Luther preached both exegetical and expository sermons. Using a theological source, explain the difference between these two forms of communication.

2. Find one of Luther's hymns. If you can sing or play an instrument, learn it and perform it for someone or for your church.

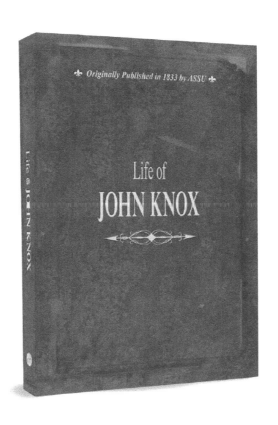

Biographical Worksheets

for Use with

Life of John Knox

| *Life of John Knox* | Introduction to Mary of Guise Pages 9-45 | Day 156 | Intro-Chapter 4 Worksheet 1 | Name |

Words to Know – Define each term in the context it is presented in the book.

extirpate

declaimed

aversion

artifice

retinue

dowager

expostualting

inconstancy

Short Answer

1. What two characteristics of Knox are stated as the most conspicuous examples of qualities that made him fit for the task of reforming Scotland (page 14)?

2. Knox first plainly perceived that the Catholic Church's doctrine had become corrupted by reading the works of which two ancient church leaders?

3. How would you describe the atmosphere in Scotland in the early days of the Reformation?

4. Why did Protestants take refuge in the castle at St. Andrews?

5. What did Knox mean when he said, "he would not run where God had not sent him"?

6. How does Knox's reaction to his call to preaching compare to that of Luther?

7. What reputation did Knox develop in his early days of preaching?

8. Why did Knox spend time in Geneva, Frankfurt, and London?

Activities

1. To provide a greater context to the issue of Christian persecution in this region, read accounts of the lives of John Wickliffe and George Wishart.

2. As you read through *Life of John Knox*, make a T-chart comparing and contrasting the life of Knox to that of German reformer Martin Luther. What similarities and differences do you see in the character and actions of these two men?

| Life of John Knox | A solemn covenant to Wicked joy Pages 45-88 | Day 159 | Chapters 5-8 Worksheet 1 | Name |

Words to Know – Define each term in the context it is presented in the book.

solicited

dauphin

effrontery

precipitation

detestation

remonstrances

reft

languid

indurate

appertains

Short Answer

1. Chapter 5 begins with an overview of the Scottish Protestants' beliefs. Summarize them.

2. Recount the details of the murder of Walter Mill. What was the broader significance of this incident?

3. What event caused the destruction of much of the church and monasteries by a mob at Perth?

4. Summarize the bold answer given by Knox at St. Andrews when threatened by the queen's army.

5. How do you feel about the fact that there was a "protestant army" that plundered Catholic monuments all over Scotland, even though, "few of the Roman Catholics were exposed to any personal insult, and not a single man suffered death"?

6. How did Knox respond to the queen's charges that he had incited rebellion, written a book against her authority, and caused sedition even in England?

7. How would you describe the relationship of Knox and the queen? How do you think he was able to be so bold in her presence?

Activities

1. This section introduces Mary, Queen of Scots, who was in many ways the archenemy of Knox in Scotland. Do some research about this unique woman to better understand the context of the following chapters.

| Life of John Knox | The assembly to End Pages 89-140 | Day 162 | Chapters 9-13 Worksheet 1 | Name |

Words to Know – Define each term in the context it is presented in the book.

indefatigable

actuated

apoplectic

contrivers

abhor

calamity

traduced

austere

thraldom

Short Answer

1. Why does the author find it "instructive" to tell the reader about the demise of Bothwell?

2. Describe how Knox was able to survive an assassination attempt in 1571.

3. In his last days, Knox found comfort in the 17th chapter of John and the 53rd chapter of Isaiah. Read these chapters and summarize their contents. Why do you think Knox wanted to hear these passages in particular?

4. How did Knox defend his severity toward those he challenged (page 118)?

5. What were the words of the earl of Morton (one of Knox's opponents) upon the death of Knox?

6. How does the author defend the severity and vehemence of Knox? Do you agree with this reasoning? Why or why not?

7. Why does the author tell us to consider the reformer more than the man when studying the Life of Knox?

8. To what biblical character does the author compare Knox?

9. Compare the lives of Knox and Luther. What similarities are found in their character? How did these factors make them suitable for the cause of the Reformation in their respective countries?

Activities

1. Research more information on the Massacre of St. Bartholomew. Can you understand why Knox was so saddened by this event?

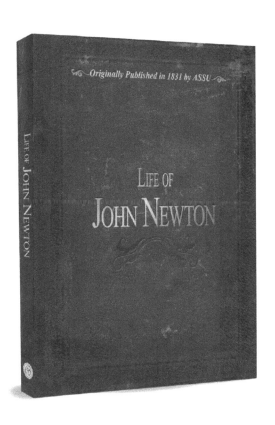

Biographical Worksheets

for Use with

Life of John Newton

| *Life of John Newton* | Biography to From Cape de Verd Pages 5-45 | Day 167 | Chapters 1-3 Worksheet 1 | Name |

Words to Know – Define each term in the context it is presented in the book.

propensities

protracted

contiguous

pittance

caprices

necromances

amulets

Short Answer

1. According to the opening pages of the book, what lessons can be learned from a study of the life of Newton?

2. Why did the loss of his mother cause young John Newton so much trouble?

3. Newton's adolescent years were spent alternating between riotous living and pious reform, but it was never long before he declined again. Why do you think this is often the case with young people? What could be learned from his example?

4. Describe the impact the other sailors had on Newton's character during his earliest days at sea.

5. By a sudden event, Newton found himself on board a new ship, the Harwich, with a chance to improve his situation. What was the result instead?

6. Describe the situation Newton found himself in when he went into the service of a slave trader in the Plantanes.

7. When finally given a chance to escape captivity and return to England, why did Newton at first seem indifferent and consider staying in Africa? Why did he finally decide to go?

8. How would you summarize the life and character of John Newton at this point in his young life?

Activities

1. Review a map of the western coast of Africa to see the places Newton journeyed to during his years at sea.
2. Read Titus 3:3. Why did Newton quote this passage in reference to his early life (page 37)?

| *Life of John Newton* | Newton's situation to After his marriage Pages 45-85 | Day 170 | Chapters 4-6 Worksheet 1 | Name |

Words to Know – Define each term in the context it is presented in the book.

circumspect

tempest

hummocks

vouchsafe

chimerical

ruminate

mirth

genteel

Short Answer

1. Newton's ship encountered a violent storm that very nearly left the whole crew dead at sea. What effect did this event have on his life?

2. By the time the ship arrived in Ireland, what had Newton decided?

3. Newton was particularly struck by three biblical passages. Read each and comment about why you think Newton was moved by these verses of Scripture.

   a. Luke 13

   b. 1 Timothy 1

   c. Luke 15

Second Semester/Fourth Quarter ⁄⁄ 107

4. Why do you think Newton constantly referred to the mercy and providence of God that protected him for all those years before he entered the ministry?

5. Upon going back to Africa, Newton ran into the mistress of his former master. Describe their interaction and what it reveals about Newton's character.

6. How does the author and Newton himself reconcile the fact that Newton was engaged in the slave trade while proclaiming the mercy of God?

7. This book was published by an American organization in 1831. How do you think that affected the statements made about slavery? What could be inferred about the author based on these facts?

Activities

1. Read the Book of Jonah. What comparisons do you see between the lives of Newton and Jonah — comparisons that led his captain to say he had "a Jonah" on board?

2. Clarkson and Wilberforce are mentioned in connection with Newton. What is the connection? How are their stories intertwined?

3. The American Colonization Society's efforts in the establishment of Liberia are mentioned briefly. Research this group and find out what their goals were and if they achieved them.

| Life of John Newton | After a short stay Pages 85-115 | Day 173 | Chapter 7 Worksheet 1 | Name |

Words to Know – Define each term in the context it is presented in the book.

diametrically

deplorable

Septuagint

opulence

concilliating

commiserate

Short Answer

1. What lesson do you learn from the story of when Newton ran into an old friend on the *Harwich*?

2. "Perhaps we have sometimes been tempted to think, that because we do not possess titles and estates and are not of high distinction and estimation in the world, we received nothing extraordinary." What two reflections does Newton make to discount this sentiment? Do you agree with him? Why or why not?

3. As noted in several instances before, it seems that God protected and preserved Newton through many close calls. This chapter includes more. Recount one of them.

4. How did Newton prepare himself for the ministry?

5. How did Newton respond to those who said his sermons were too short?

Activities

1. Though his writing of hymns is only briefly mentioned in this text, Newton is best known today for penning the classic hymn, "Amazing Grace." Now that you know his story, read through the lyrics of the song. Write a poem or short narrative that fuses the lyrics of the song with the facts of Newton's life.

Life of John Newton | After a short stay to End Pages 115-144 | Day 176 | Chapter 7 Worksheet 2 | Name

Words to Know – Define each term in the context it is presented in the book.

dogmatical

unequivocal

probity

pillory

avocations

impertinent

perspicuous

jocular

Short Answer

1. Summarize the main point of the sermon excerpted on pages 116–121. Why is this an important message?

2. What did Newton mean when he said, "Tell me not how the man died, but how he lived"?

3. What warning is given to the reader when considering the life of John Newton (page 128)?

4. What were Newton's strengths and weaknesses as a minister?

5. What point was Newton making when he said, "I am considered as an Arminian among the high Calvinists, and as a Calvinist among the strenuous Arminians"?

6. In your opinion, what is the greatest lesson that can be learned from the life of John Newton?

Activities

1. Newton lived just long enough to witness the passage of the Slave Trade Act of 1807. Research this law and the effects that it had on slavery around the world (including the United States).

2. Newton was skilled at finding spiritual truths from "even the basest materials," and would then use them for sermon illustrations. In his own words, "A minister, wherever he is, should be always in his study. He should look at every man, and at everything, as capable of affording him some instruction." This week, do the same. Find something commonplace that could be used as a spiritual illustration. Share your lesson with someone.

Quizzes & Tests Section

Life of Washington
Concepts & Comprehension — Quiz 1
Scope: Chapters 1-3 **Total score:** ____ of 100 **Name:** _____

Vocabulary: (2 Points Each Answer)

anecdote   filial   prudent   pecuniary   approbation   resolute
veneration   sundry   huzzahing   unostentatiously

1. _____: very determined; having or showing a lot of determination.
2. _____: the act of expressing a shout of acclaim — often used to express joy
3. _____: an act of approving formally or officially
4. _____: marked by wisdom or good judgment
5. _____: respect or awe inspired by the dignity, wisdom, or talent of a person
6. _____: of various kinds; several
7. _____: consisting of or measured in money
8. _____: of or relating to a son or daughter; appropriate for a son or daughter.
9. _____: a short and amusing or interesting story about a real incident or person.
10. _____: refusing to display wealth, knowledge, etc., in a way that is meant to attract attention, admiration, or envy.

Short Answer: (10 Points Each Blank)

11. Describe the importance of Washington's relationship with his mother.

12. What does it say about Washington's character that "those who were nearest to him, and knew him best, loved him most"?

13. Describe the response of Washington to his appointment as commander-in-chief.

14. In the first year of the Revolutionary War, the Americans saw little success. How did this affect morale, and how did Washington deal with this issue?

15. Describe the miraculous way in which Washington was able to capture 1,000 men at Trenton with only the loss of two of his own men.

16. What revolutionary action did Washington take to protect his army from smallpox?

Long Answer: (20 Points Each Question)

17. "I shall never forget what I felt when I saw him brave all the danger of the field . . . he is surely in heaven's peculiar care."

    Based on what you have read so far (chapters 1–3), describe three incidents that could be used as evidence to support this assertion about Washington's divine protection.

| Q | *Life of Washington* Concepts & Comprehension | Quiz 2 | Scope: Chapters 5-6 | Total score: ____ of 100 | Name |

Vocabulary: (2 Points Each Answer)

fidelity   miscreant   impious   wanton   repine   sloop   conflagration
imprecations   mutiny   dissipation

1. _____: a war or conflict
2. _____: the quality or state of being faithful
3. _____: a small sailboat with one mast
4. _____: wasteful expenditure, intemperate living; excessive drinking
5. _____: feeling or showing a lack of respect for God; not pious
6. _____: curses
7. _____: to feel or express dejection or discontent; complain.
8. _____: one who behaves criminally or viciously
9. _____: showing no thought or care for the rights, feelings, or safety of others
10. _____: a situation in which a group of people (such as sailors or soldiers) refuses to obey orders and try to take control away from the person who commands them

Short Answer: (10 Points Each Blank)

11. Describe Washington's dining habits at Valley Forge. What do they reveal about his character?

12. The text describes three eyewitness accounts of Washington's devotion to prayer. Describe at least one of these accounts.

13. How did Washington's prayer life reflect the truth of Matthew 6:6?

14. Describe the order issued by Washington to his troops on July 29, 1779.

15. Pages 141–153 share the story of how Benedict Arnold became the nation's most famous traitor. In the space below, briefly recount what led to this infamy.

16. Recount the story of what happened when Washington's home was facing the threat of being burned by the British. What was Washington's response, and what does that reveal about his character?

Long Answer: (20 Points Each Question)

17. Page 152 talks about "chance" and "accidents." Based on what you've learned from this text, does it appear to you that the ultimate success of the Americans was due to just "chance," or do you think it was the Providence of God? Use specific events to explain.

Life of Washington
Concepts & Comprehension — Quiz 3
Scope: Chapters 8-11
Total score: ____ of 100
Name

Vocabulary: (2 Points Each Answer)

eminence   deportment   diffidence   rectitude   felicity   concourse
tranquility   homage   privateer   insolent

1. _____: respect, honor
2. _____: the quality or state of being right, moral integrity
3. _____: rude or impolite; having or showing a lack of respect for others
4. _____: an armed private ship licensed to attack enemy shipping
5. _____: an area of high ground
6. _____: a meeting produced by voluntary or spontaneous coming together
7. _____: the quality or state of being happy
8. _____: being hesitant in acting or speaking through lack of self-confidence
9. _____: the quality or state of being at peace
10. _____: the way that a person behaves, stands, and moves, especially in a formal situation

Short Answer: (10 Points Each Blank)

11. As Cornwallis and his men marched out of Yorktown in defeat, how did Washington address his men?

12. A few new recruits marched to Philadelphia and demanded that Congress pay them within twenty minutes. Describe Washington's reaction when he heard this news.

13. According to the text, how should you view your freedom?

14. Describe Washington's response to his election as president.

15. What was the main source of trouble during Washington's second term in office, what was his strategy for dealing with it, and why did he choose that strategy?

16. In 1794, the Whiskey Rebellion erupted in western Pennsylvania. What was it about, and what was Washington's response?

Long Answer: (20 Points Each Question)

17. Both chapters 10 and 11 share stories of Washington's encounters with ordinary citizens. In light of these anecdotes, what could be said about the feelings of the American people toward him and his relationship with them?

| **Q** | *Life of Washington*
Concepts & Comprehension | Quiz 4 | Scope:
Chapters 12–End | Total score:
____ of 100 | Name |

Vocabulary: (2 Points Each Answer)

idleness   dispositions   indigent   frank   trifling   benefactor   inculcated
abhorrence   proffered   solicitude

1. _____: the attitudes or moods of a person
2. _____: of little importance; trivial
3. _____: one that confers a benefit; especially one that makes a gift
4. _____: implanted by repeated statement or admonition
5. _____: suffering from extreme poverty
6. _____: concern that someone feels about someone's health or happiness
7. _____: put before a person for acceptance; offered
8. _____: a feeling of disgust
9. _____: an inclination not to do work or engage in activities
10. _____: a signature or mark affixed by special privilege to a letter, package, or the like to ensure its transmission free of charge, as by mail.

Short Answer: (10 Points Each Blank)

11. According to pages 246–247, what role did Washington think religion should play in politics?

12. Give a specific example of how Washington cared for the poor.

13. Washington was called on once again to lead the American military in 1798. What led to this?

14. Briefly recount the events culminating in Washington's death.

Long Answer: (20 Points Each Question)

15. Many contemporary scholars suggest that Washington was not a Christian, or at best was only a deist. Based on the evidence given in this book (particularly in the conclusion), refute that conclusion.

16. The author closes with, "Was he not worthy of your imitation?" Giving specific examples, answer this question.

| Q | *Life of Andrew Jackson* Concepts & Comprehension | Quiz 5 | Scope: Chapters 1-3 | Total score: ____of 100 | Name |

Vocabulary: (2 Points Each Answer)

incipient   habiliments   assuage   churlishness   provocation   morose   affability
privations   censure   torpor

1. _____: friendliness
2. _____: very serious, unhappy, and quiet; gloomy
3. _____: an official act of reprimand or condemnation
4. _____: a state of not being active and having very little energy
5. _____: the dress characteristic of an occupation or occasion; clothing
6. _____: beginning to develop or exist
7. _____: impoliteness; vulgarity
8. _____: to make (something, such as an unpleasant feeling) less painful or severe
9. _____: an action or occurrence that causes someone to become angry
10. _____: a lack or loss of the basic things that people need to live properly

Short Answer: (10 Points Each Blank)

11. What do you think the author meant by this statement: "Whatever may be the views entertained in regard to his merits as a warrior, or his abilities as a statesman, his conduct in both capacities was such as must necessarily command attention"?

12. Describe the incident that left a scar on Jackson's left hand.

13. As a budding lawyer on the western frontier, Jackson made 22 trips into the dangerous backwoods country of Tennessee. What do we learn about the character of Jackson during this time?

14. How did Jackson end up in his infamous duel with Charles Dickinson? What does this event reveal about Jackson's character?

15. What did Jackson do once he found out that his partner in business had racked up more debt than he could afford? What does this tell you about Jackson?

16. Jackson is notable for fostering a fierce loyalty from those who served him. Based on what you have learned so far, why do you think that was the case?

Long Answer: (20 Points Each Question)

17. In *Life of Washington*, we discussed the type of sterling reputation Washington had developed by the time he was chosen to lead the Continental Army. Compare and contrast that reputation with the reputation Jackson had developed by a similar age. In what ways are they similar, and in what ways are they different?

Life of Andrew Jackson
Concepts & Comprehension

Quiz 6 — Scope: Chapters 4-6 — Total score: ____ of 100 — Name

Vocabulary: (2 Points Each Answer)

accoutrements lassitude trepidation chagrined amicable prevaricate
satiety intrepidity auspiciously ardor

1. _____: the condition of being tired; lack of physical or mental energy
2. _____: a feeling of fear that causes you to hesitate
3. _____: to avoid telling the truth by not directly answering a question
4. _____: strength of mind to carry on in spite of danger
5. _____: accessory items of clothing or equipment
6. _____: characterized by friendly goodwill; peaceable
7. _____: a feeling or condition of being full after eating food.
8. _____: showing or suggesting that future success is likely
9. _____: energy, enthusiasm, or passion
10. _____: frustrated or annoyed because of failure or disappointment

Short Answer: (10 Points Each Blank)

11. What happened to the orphaned Indian boy at the Battle of Tallushatchee? Does this reveal anything significant about the character of Andrew Jackson?

12. Most of chapter 5 deals with the difficulties Jackson faced in obtaining food for his men. As a result, they attempted mutiny several times. Using several examples from the chapter, explain how Jackson was able to keep his men from leaving.

13. How would you describe the leadership displayed by Jackson during this trying time? What characteristics were admirable? Where there any characteristics that were not so admirable? Would you have handled it differently?

14. According to the text, Jackson was often very generous when taking care of those in less-fortunate circumstances. How could the charity of Jackson be compared to Washington?

15. What happened to the young Indian wounded in the battle near Tohopeka?

16. Based on what you've read, do you think Jackson's assault of Pensacola was justified? Give reasons to support your answer.

Long Answer: (20 Points Each Question)

17. Colonel Milton asked Captain Gordon what sort of man General Jackson was. What was Captain Gordon's answer? How did Milton respond to Gordon's answer? How would you answer the question, "What sort of man was General Jackson?"

| Q | *Life of Andrew Jackson* Concepts & Comprehension | Quiz 7 | Scope: Chapters 7-9 | Total score: ____of 100 | Name |

Vocabulary: (2 Points Each Answer)

alacrity   assiduity   conjecture   judicious   galled   nefarious   impervious
licentious   incessant   glacis

1. _____: not allowing entrance or passage; impenetrable
2. _____: a quick and cheerful readiness to do something
3. _____: flagrantly wicked or impious
4. _____: diligence
5. _____: having or showing good judgment
6. _____: an opinion or idea formed without proof or sufficient evidence
7. _____: continuing without stopping; not stopping
8. _____: a slope that runs downward from a fortification
9. _____: vexed or irritated greatly
10. _____: sexually immoral or offensive

Short Answer: (10 Points Each Blank)

11. What is "martial law," and why did Jackson put New Orleans under it?

12. Although the Americans had very decided advantages, at the end of the night (on December 23) Jackson chose not to pursue and conquer the enemy. How did he come to this difficult conclusion?

13. According to the text, what were the distinguishing traits in the character of General Jackson as a military commander?

14. What did Jackson mean when he said, "The surest defence, and one which seldom failed of success, was a rampart of high-minded and brave men"?

15. The author states, "It was impossible for men to serve under such a leader as Jackson, without becoming imbued with the same dauntless courage which he always exhibited." Why do you think Jackson was able to do this?

16. What was the author implying when he stated that the general "seldom slept: he was always at his post, performing the duties of both general and soldier"?

Long Answer: (20 Points Each Question)

17. Chapters 7–9 all deal with the strategic actions taken by Jackson in order to defend New Orleans. Carefully explain why the Americans were able to defeat a much larger and superior British army.

Life of Andrew Jackson | Concepts & Comprehension | Quiz 8 | Scope: Chapters 10-12 | Total score: ____ of 100 | Name

Vocabulary: (2 Points Each Answer)

encomium asperity temerity averred plenipotentiary rapine parlance
celerity incendiaries writ of habeas corpus

1. _____: pillage or plunder
2. _____: unreasonable or foolhardy contempt of danger or opposition
3. _____: glowing and warmly enthusiastic praise
4. _____: invested with full power
5. _____: verified or proven to be true in pleading a cause
6. _____: language used by a particular group of people
7. _____: verified or proven to be true in pleading a cause
8. _____: rapidity of motion or action
9. _____: harshness of behavior or speech that expresses bitterness or anger
10. _____: a court order that requires a person under arrest to be brought to court

Short Answer: (10 Points Each Blank)

11. What happened after Jackson received a $1,000 fine from Judge Hall?

12. Why is Jackson often referred to as Old Hickory?

13. The text says that Jackson's "opinions could not be changed, and the line of conduct he had marked out was fixed and unalterable." Would you consider this a good or bad quality for a leader to have? Explain.

14. The election of 1824 has become known in history as the "Corrupt Bargain." Though this text doesn't explicitly use that terminology, explain why Jackson supporters came up with this label.

15. How did Jackson respond to Mr. Randolph's attempted assault?

16. Summarize Jackson's religious statements made on his deathbed.

Long Answer: (20 Points Each Question)

17. Pages 191–193 make the case that Jackson was no ordinary man, and in many respects could be considered one of the most remarkable men who ever lived. Summarize the evidence given for this argument.

| Q | *Life of Luther* Concepts & Comprehension | Quiz 9 | Scope: Part 1, Chs 1-3 | Total score: ____ of 100 | Name |

Vocabulary: (2 Points Each Answer)

declivity   turbid   cogitations   penury   pensive   capacious   mendicant
vitiated   demure   genuflection

1. _____: cloudy or muddy
2. _____: someone who lives by asking people for money or food
3. _____: made less effective; ruined or spoiled
4. _____: the act of bowing on a knee in worship or awe
5. _____: thoughts or careful reflections
6. _____: a downward slope
7. _____: able to hold or contain a lot; large in capacity
8. _____: quiet, modest, and polite
9. _____: quietly sad or thoughtful
10. _____: extreme poverty

Short Answer: (10 Points Each Blank)

11. How does the author describe the state of the Catholic Church at the time of Luther's education?

12. What effects did Luther's mother have on her son?

13. Describe Luther's first encounter with a Bible. How was Luther able to go into adulthood without ever seeing a Bible? What does this tell you about the nature of the Church at this time in history?

14. What two ideas did Luther first began to explore at Erfurt — ideas that would later be the backbone of the Reformation?

15. Generally speaking, why did Luther consider becoming a monk? Specifically, what incident led him to make a vow to become a monk?

16. Describe the monastic process of biblical interpretation as outlined in this chapter.

Long Answer: (20 Points Each Question)

17. How did Luther's socio-economic background and geographic location benefit his efforts to reform the Church?

| Q | *Life of Luther* Concepts & Comprehension | Quiz 10 | Scope: Part 1, Chs 3.2-4 | Total score: ____ of 100 | Name |

Vocabulary: (2 Points Each Answer)

lucre   cumbrous   mien   exculpate   ablution   erudite   decorous
pernicious   ignominiously   obstreperous

1. _____: the washing of one's body or part of it (as in a religious rite)
2. _____: hard to manage or handle
3. _____: correct and polite in a particular situation
4. _____: marked with or characterized by disgrace or shame; dishonorably
5. _____: stubbornly resistant to control; unruly
6. _____: a person's appearance or facial expression
7. _____: monetary gain; profit
8. _____: having or showing knowledge that is learned by studying
9. _____: to prove that someone is not guilty of doing something wrong
10. _____: causing great harm often in a way that is not easily seen or noticed

Short Answer: (10 Points Each Blank)

11. Why is Luther's relationship with Staupitz described as "the most important acquaintance which Luther ever formed"?

12. Why was Luther very concerned about becoming a priest?

13. Pages 114–115 lay out basic differences between the Catholic and Protestant faiths. Summarize the contents of this section.

14. Why was Luther's study of Greek and Hebrew crucial to his spiritual formation?

15. Why was the oath that Luther took upon receiving his doctor of divinity an important part of Luther's later defense of the Reformation?

16. In 1509, Luther was called upon to begin preaching. He was extremely reluctant. How did he overcome this? What spiritual lessons could be learned from this incident?

Long Answer: (20 Points Each Question)

17. Much of this section is given to quotations of letters written by Luther. The purpose is to present to you a picture of how Luther had developed by the time the Reformation began. With that in mind, summarize the social, intellectual, and theological changes that had taken hold of Luther by early 1517.

| Q | *Life of Luther* Concepts & Comprehension | Quiz 11 | Scope: Part 2, Chapter 1 | Total score: ____ of 100 | Name |

Vocabulary: (2 Points Each Answer)

plenary   transient   magnanimity   fulminate   odium   corpulent   promulgated
puerile   servile   supercilious

1. _____: to complain loudly or angrily
2. _____: disrepute or infamy attached to something; opprobrium
3. _____: fat
4. _____: very obedient and trying too hard to please someone
5. _____: complete in every respect, absolute, unqualified
6. _____: not lasting long
7. _____: made known to many people
8. _____: childish, juvenile, or silly
9. _____: coolly and patronizingly haughty
10. _____: loftiness of spirit enabling one to bear trouble calmly, to disdain meanness and pettiness, and to display a noble generosity

Short Answer: (10 Points Each Blank)

11. Describe the role that indulgences had come to play in the church by Luther's time.

12. What three successful acts were required for absolution of sin? What were Luther's primary concerns with this process of absolution?

13. What evidence exists to suggest that Luther wasn't really trying to instigate a public rebellion with his 95 theses? Why did he publish a simpler version of his arguments?

14. Rather than buy indulgences, how did Luther suggest that Christians should spend their money? Why? How did Luther deal with members of his own congregation who presented him with their indulgences?

15. At this point in Luther's life (mid-1518), how would you describe Luther's relation with the Catholic Church? Was he still loyal, or had he already made up his mind to break away?

16. Page 241 contains this quote from Luther: "Still, I sincerely regard ecclesiastical authority." Considering the context, do you think he was being completely sincere? Explain.

Long Answer: (20 Points Each Question)

17. The author states, "Luther was not perfect, was not always consistent, nor always right either in his opinions or in his feelings. Far from it." Provide evidence to support this statement.

| Q | *Life of Luther* Concepts & Comprehension | Quiz 12 | Scope: Part 2, Chs 2-4.1 | Total score: ____of 100 | Name |

Vocabulary: (2 Points Each Answer)

jocosely   aspersion   escutcheon   disingenuous   spurious   sycophancy
perfidious   gesticulation   garrulity   iota

1. _____: a sprinkling with water, especially in religious ceremonies
2. _____: cheerfully; jokingly
3. _____: self-seeking flattery
4. _____: pointlessly or annoyingly talkative
5. _____: not able to be trusted
6. _____: the act of making expressive gestures
7. _____: not genuine, sincere, or authentic
8. _____: giving the false appearance of being honest or sincere
9. _____: a shield or emblem bearing a coat of arms
10. _____: a very small amount

Short Answer: (10 Points Each Blank)

11. What were the consequences of the great debate at Leipsic?

12. After the debate, Luther was very busy with scholarly writing. What work of his is considered the "chief work" in which the fundamental principles of the Reformation are laid down?

13. What did Luther expect from the Diet of Worms? What does it say about his character that he went anyway?

14. What admirable qualities do you see in the way Luther handled his interrogation at the Diet of Worms?

15. What new problems and questions arose from the beginning of the Reformation and threatened to halt its momentum?

16. What was the main issue dividing Luther and Carlstadt?

Long Answer: (20 Points Each Question)

17. With as much detail as possible, recount the events that transpired at the Diet of Worms. Give special attention to Luther's statements and actions.

| Q | *Life of Luther* Concepts & Comprehension | Quiz 13 | Scope: Part 2, Chs 4.3-5 | Total score: ____ of 100 | Name |

Vocabulary: (2 Points Each Answer)

castigate circumlocution avarice fetters harangued ribaldry pertinacity
dissimulation inveterate expostulation

1. _____: excessive or insatiable desire for wealth or gain; greediness, cupidity
2. _____: use of crude, indecent, or offensive speech
3. _____: chains or shackles; restraints
4. _____: deceiving someone with false information
5. _____: disagreeing with something or arguing against it
6. _____: always or often happening or existing
7. _____: lectured; gave a speech to a large assembly
8. _____: the quality of being persistent and tenacious
9. _____: to subject to severe punishment, reproof, or criticism
10. _____: the use of an unnecessarily large number of words to express an idea

Short Answer: (10 Points Each Blank)

11. "Luther never loved those who taught differently than himself. . . . This was a fault in his character." Examine this statement (found on page 367) and explain why you think Luther was this way. What might have been different had Luther been more beneficent toward his opposition?

12. "He was a better theologian than politician." What was the circumstance that led the author to make this criticism of Luther?

13. Describe the way Luther handled money.

14. Why did Luther hesitate to take a wife, even though he now had the freedom of conscience to do so?

15. Describe the qualities that made Luther an excellent orator and preacher.

16. Why was Luther such a strong supporter of public education? How does this figure prominently into the Reformation? According to Luther, what role should parents play in the education of their children?

Long Answer: (20 Points Each Question)

17. Based on everything you have learned about the life of Luther, what qualities made him a likely candidate to bring about the Reformation? What qualities made him an unlikely candidate?

| Q | *Life of John Knox* Concepts & Comprehension | Quiz 14 | Scope: Chapters 1-13 | Total score: ____ of 100 | Name |

Vocabulary: (2 Points Each Answer)

retinue   effrontery   languid   indurate   dauphin   indefatigable
thralldom   actuated   apoplectic   artifice

1. _____: shameless boldness; insolence
2. _____: the state of being a slave
3. _____: physically or morally hardened
4. _____: a group of helpers, supporters, or followers
5. _____: incapable of being fatigued; untiring
6. _____: dishonest behavior or speech that is meant to deceive someone
7. _____: caused to do something or to act in a certain way
8. _____: the eldest son of a king
9. _____: showing or having very little strength, energy, or activity
10. _____: affected with, inclined to, or showing symptoms of stroke

Short Answer: (10 Points Each Blank)

11. What two characteristics of Knox are stated as the most conspicuous examples of qualities that made him fit for the task of reforming Scotland?

12. Chapter 5 begins with an overview of the Scottish Protestants' beliefs. Summarize them.

13. Why does the author tell us to consider *the reformer* more than the man when studying the *Life of Knox*?

14. How does Knox's reaction to his call to preaching compare to that of Luther?

15. How would you describe the relationship of Knox and the queen? How do you think he was able to be so bold in her presence?

16. How does the author defend the severity and vehemence of Knox? Do you agree with this reasoning? Why or why not?

Long Answer: (20 Points Each Question)

17. Compare the lives of Knox and Luther. What similarities are found in their character? How did these factors make them suitable for the cause of the Reformation in their respective countries?

| Q *Life of John Newton* Concepts & Comprehension | Quiz 15 | Scope: Chapters 1-7 | Total score: ____ of 100 | Name |

Vocabulary: (2 Points Each Answer)

commiserate   mirth   caprices   probity   perspicuous

1. _____: sudden changes in mood or behavior
2. _____: the quality of a person who is completely honest
3. _____: to feel or express sympathy
4. _____: gladness or gaiety as shown by or accompanied with laughter
5. _____; plain to the understanding, especially because of clarity and precision of presentation

Short Answer: (10 Points Each Blank)

6. Why do you think Newton constantly referred to the mercy and providence of God that protected him for all those years before he entered the ministry?

7. What were Newton's strengths and weaknesses as a minister?

8. As noted in several instances throughout the book, it seems that God, by His divine providence, protected and preserved Newton through many close calls. Provide at least two examples of this.

Long Answer: (20 Points Each Question)

9. Write a biographical sketch of the life of John Newton. Include as many details as you call recall, paying special attention to his life before and after his conversion. What spiritual lessons can we learn from a study of his life?

| **T** | *Life of Washington* Concepts & Comprehension | Test 1 | Scope: Complete Book | Total score: ____ of 100 | Name |

Vocabulary: (2 Points Each Answer)

frank   eminence   trifling   diffidence   veneration   pecuniary   approbation
repine   conflagration   imprecations

1. _____: of little importance; trivial
2. _____: an area of high ground
3. _____: consisting of or measured in money
4. _____: an act of approving formally or officially
5. _____: to feel or express dejection or discontent; complain.
6. _____: curses
7. _____: being hesitant in acting or speaking through lack of self-confidence
8. _____: a war or conflict
9. _____: respect or awe inspired by the dignity, wisdom, or talent of a person
10. _____: a signature or mark affixed by special privilege to a letter, package, or the like to ensure its transmission free of charge, as by mail.

Long Answer: (20 Points Each Question)

11. The book asserts that Washington was protected by the Providence of God — what some may explain as "chance" or "coincidence." Based on what you've learned from this text, does it appear to you that the ultimate success of Washington and the Americans cause was due to just "chance," or do you think it was the Providence of God? Use specific events to explain.

12. Washington is considered one of our greatest national leaders. What specific characteristics made him such a great leader? Use specific information to answer.

13. The author closes with, "Was he not worthy of your imitation?" Giving specific examples, answer this question.

14. Many contemporary scholars suggest that Washington was not a Christian, or at best was only a deist. Based on the evidence given in this book (particularly in the conclusion), refute that conclusion.

| **T** | *Life of Andrew Jackson* Concepts & Comprehension | Test 2 | Scope: Complete Book | Total score: ____ of 100 | Name |

Vocabulary: (2 Points Each Answer)

rapine   parlance   censure   habiliments   privations   amicable
prevaricate   assiduity   alacrity   plenipotentiary

1. _____: an official act of reprimand or condemnation
2. _____: the dress characteristic of an occupation or occasion; clothing
3. _____: a lack or loss of the basic things that people need to live properly
4. _____: characterized by friendly goodwill; peaceable
5. _____: to avoid telling the truth by not directly answering a question
6. _____: diligence
7. _____: a quick and cheerful readiness to do something
8. _____: invested with full power
9. _____: language used by a particular group of people
10. _____: pillage or plunder

Long Answer: (20 Points Each Question)

11. The preface of the book contains this statement: "Whatever may be the views entertained in regard to his merits as a warrior, or his abilities as a statesman, his conduct in both capacities was such as must necessarily command attention." Now having read the book, explain why and how this statement is an accurate reflection of Andrew Jackson.

12. Chapters 7–9 all deal with the strategic actions taken by Jackson in order to defend New Orleans. Carefully explain why the Americans were able to defeat a much larger and superior British army.

13. This book makes the case that Jackson was no ordinary man, and in many respects could be considered one of the most remarkable men who ever lived. Summarize the evidence given for this argument.

14. Both George Washington and Andrew Jackson were extraordinary leaders. However, their leadership skills and traits were quite different. In the space below, compare and contrast the leadership styles of the two. Use specific examples you learned from this course.

| T | *Life of Luther* Concepts & Comprehension | Test 3 | Scope: Complete Book | Total score: ____ of 100 | Name |

Vocabulary: (2 Points Each Answer)

penury   capacious   erudite   pernicious   ignominiously   fulminate   plenary
perfidious   garrulity   ribaldry

1. _____: able to hold or contain a lot; large in capacity
2. _____: to complain loudly or angrily
3. _____: marked with or characterized by disgrace or shame; dishonorably
4. _____: complete in every respect; absolute, unqualified
5. _____: having or showing knowledge that is learned by studying
6. _____: use of crude, indecent, or offensive speech
7. _____: pointlessly or annoyingly talkative
8. _____: not able to be trusted
9. _____: extreme poverty
10. _____: causing great harm, often in a way that is not easily seen or noticed

Long Answer: (20 Points Each Question)

11. Pages 114–115 lays out basic differences between the Catholic and Protestant faiths. Summarize these differences, paying special attention to the factors that Luther preached most ardently.

12. How did Luther's socio-economic background and geographic location benefit his efforts to reform the church?

13. With as much detail as possible, recount the events that transpired at the Diet of Worms. Give special attention to Luther's statements and actions.

14. Based on everything you have learned about the life of Luther, what qualities made him a likely candidate to bring about the Reformation? What qualities made him an unlikely candidate?

| | *Life of Knox and Newton* Concepts & Comprehension | Test 4 | Scope: Complete Books | Total score: ____of 100 | Name |

Vocabulary: (2 Points Each Answer)

commiserate   mirth   caprices   probity   indefatigable   languid
thralldom   indurate retinue   effrontery

1. _____: sudden changes in mood or behavior
2. _____: incapable of being fatigued; untiring
3. _____: the state of being a slave
4. _____: shameless boldness; insolence
5. _____: gladness or gaiety as shown by or accompanied with laughter
6. _____: to feel or express sympathy
7. _____: physically or morally hardened
8. _____: a group of helpers, supporters, or followers
9. _____: the quality of a person who is completely honest
10. _____: showing or having very little strength, energy, or activity

Long Answer: (20 Points Each Question)

11. How does the author defend the severity and vehemence of Knox? Do you agree with this reasoning? Why or why not?

12. Compare the lives of Knox and Luther. What similarities are found in their character? How did these factors make them suitable for the cause of the Reformation in their respective countries?

13. As noted in several instances throughout, it seems that God, by His divine providence, protected and preserved Newton through many close calls. Provide at least two examples of this.

14. Write a short biographical sketch of the life of John Newton. What spiritual lessons can we learn from a study of his life?

Answer Keys

Life of Washington — Worksheet Answer Keys

Worksheet 1 Answer Key:

Vocabulary

indulgence: the behavior or attitude of people who allow themselves to do what they want or who allow other people to do what they want.

midshipmen: a member of the Royal Navy ranking below a lieutenant but above a basic deck hand

ascertain: to learn or find out (something, such as information or the truth).

anecdote: a short and amusing or interesting story about a real incident or person.

filial: of or relating to a son or daughter; appropriate for a son or daughter.

aide-de-camp: French for field assistant; a personal assistant to a person of high rank

Short answer

1. Answers will vary, but should focus on a close personal relationship. His mother taught him the importance of truthfulness.
2. The war began as a result of competing land claims in the Ohio River Valley. Washington marched out into the wilderness to negotiate with the French on behalf of Virginia, but those negotiations eventually turned into armed conflict.
3. Answers will vary, but should indicate that reputations are earned by our actions, and good reputation will often be rewarded.
4. Washington fought valiantly, but also managed to win favorable terms of surrender for his men.
5. British officers of lower rank were being placed over colonial officers. Washington resigned in protest of this unjust treatment.
6. Braddock ordered his troops to cross the river against Washington's recommendation. As a result, they were ambushed by the French and Indians and suffered a humiliating defeat. Braddock was mortally wounded in the attacks.
7. Washington and his horse were riddled with bullets, but he managed to escape without serious injury.
8. Christians should give to the needy, and it is honorable to God to give quietly and anonymously. When Washington paid for the bread for the needy, he wasn't seeking the attention of men but the approval of God.
9. Answers will vary, but should address the importance of character and integrity.
10. Answers will vary, but should connect lessons learned in early life to usefulness later on in life.

Worksheet 2 Answer Key:

Vocabulary

resolute: very determined; having or showing a lot of determination.

magistrate: a civil officer charged with the administration of the law.

unanimity: agreement by all people in a given situation

unostentatiously: refusing to display wealth, knowledge, etc., in a way that is meant to attract attention, admiration, or envy.

huzzahing: the act of expressing a shout of acclaim — often used interjectionally to express joy

heretofore: until this time; up until now

prudent: marked by wisdom or good judgment

approbation: an act of approving formally or officially

pecuniary: consisting of or measured in money

Short Answer

1. Answers will vary, but should compare the present spiritual condition of our nation to that of the nation in the 1770s.
2. Answers will vary, but should address the public nature of his faith.
3. His strong opinions against the taxation of Parliament earned him the title
4. The firmness of his temper, the dignity of his manners, and the confidence which was felt in his integrity and patriotism.

5. He was very humble, insisting that he wasn't qualified for such a high post, and refused to be paid for his work.

6. Answers should reflect the truth of each of these Scriptures:
   a. Ephesians 4:26
   b. James 1:19–20
   c. Ecclesiastes 7:9
   d. Proverbs 22:24–25
   e. Proverbs 29:11

Worksheet 3 Answer Key:

Vocabulary

veneration: respect or awe inspired by the dignity, wisdom, dedication, or talent of a person

melancholy: sadness or depression of the spirits; gloom

sundry: of various kinds; several

candour (candor): the quality of being open and honest in expression; frankness

imputation: insinuation

presumption: behavior perceived as arrogant, disrespectful, and transgressing the limits of what is permitted or appropriate.

mortification: a sense of humiliation and shame caused by something that wounds one's pride or self-respect

imprudently: lacking discretion, wisdom, or good judgment

Tories: Americans upholding the cause of the British Crown against the supporters of colonial independence during the American Revolution; loyalists

Short Answer

1. Answers will vary, but should indicate the need of divine intervention in the task before the founders.

2. General Howe did not address him correctly as "commander-in-chief." Washington also believed that in his position, he had not been given the authority to act in that manner. This shows us that he was not given to the abuse of power.

3. Morale was low. Washington had to take on the role of chief encourager.

4. "On our part the war should be defensive; we should, on all occasions, avoid a general action; nor put anything to the risk, unless compelled by necessity, into which we ought never to be drawn."

5. A dense fog rolled in that facilitated their escape, even though the enemy was only a few hundred yards away.

6. His men crossed the icy Delaware River on Christmas night and surprise attacked the men on the other side.

7. He had them all inoculated, which had never been done on such a large scale.

8. Answers will vary, but the examples should describe incidents where the protective hand of God was upon Washington and his men.

Worksheet 4 Answer Key:

Vocabulary

repine: to feel or express dejection or discontent; complain

inclinations: feelings of wanting to do something; a tendency to do something

miscreant: one who behaves criminally or viciously

fidelity: the quality or state of being faithful

impious: feeling or showing a lack of respect for God; not pious

abominable: worthy of or causing disgust or hatred; quite disagreeable or unpleasant

imprecations: curses

wanton: showing no thought or care for the rights, feelings, or safety of others

Short Answer

1. He said he would joyfully resign if asked to, but that he would not "shrink from the cause" until that point.

2. Washington was willing to eat the same poor provisions as his men — hard bread and a few potatoes. Answers will vary on part two.

3. No amount of money could convince him to seek peace without the promise of American independence as one of the conditions.

4. He didn't let them affect his actions. He continued to faithfully discharge the duties of his office. He let his character speak for itself.

5. All three accounts speak of Washington withdrawing privately to engage in prayer.

6. He prayed to his Father in secret, and his Father rewarded him with success against great odds.

7. Washington played the role of peacemaker, exchanging letters with the offended parties until things were smoothed over.

8. He was implying that God's hand was so obviously upon the Americans that anyone who couldn't see it must not even believe in God.

9. The order was for soldiers to be punished for excessive swearing — particularly the use of God's name in vain.

10. Answers will vary, but should indicate that Washington was concerned about having the favor of God upon their efforts.

Worksheet 5 Answer Key:

Vocabulary

dissipation: wasteful expenditure, intemperate living; especially excessive drinking

depraved: very evil; having or showing an evil and immoral character

sloop: a small sailboat with one mast

deluded: mislead in the mind or judgment

mutiny: a situation in which a group of people (such as sailors or soldiers) refuse to obey orders and try to take control away from the person who commands them

impropriety: rude or immoral behavior: improper behavior

conflagration: a war or conflict

Short Answer

1. Arnold wasted much money and as a result tried to give up West Point to the British in return for a high commission in the British Army. His plans were foiled, but he did manage to escape and join the ranks of the British.

2. Answers will vary.

3. Answers will vary, but should describe the fact that nothing happens without the direction of the sovereign God. The many miraculous escapes of the Americans are very hard to explain away as simple accidents.

4. He determined that the British had no chance of defeating a group of people who were willing to nearly go hungry in order to defend their liberty.

5. He made all the preparations necessary to subdue them, but refused to interfere directly unless it did become violent. He let his subordinates handle it. Yet he also used this incident to convince Congress to contribute to their relief.

6. Cornwallis underestimated Lafayette because of his youth.

7. The man who was watching Washington's home chose to give provisions to the men threatening the fire rather than see the property destroyed. Washington was upset, saying that he'd rather see his home burned than cooperate with the enemy. He said it set a bad example. Answers will vary on part two.

8. He didn't want to do anything that was only good for his state and not good for all of the states.

9. The best things in life are often found in the darkest of circumstances. Answers will vary on part two, but should include a personal example of this profound truth.

10. He loaned, from his personal finances, a sum of $1.4 million to the government in order to provide salaries and provisions for the troops.

Worksheet 6 Answer Key:

Vocabulary

eminence: an area of high ground

posterity: all future generations

deportment: the way that a person behaves, stands, and moves, especially in a formal situation

felicity: the quality or state of being happy

ardently: eagerly and zealously

procured: received (something) by some action or effort

diffidence: the quality of being hesitant in acting or speaking through lack of self-confidence

rectitude: the quality or state of being right; moral integrity

sanguine: confident, optimistic

august body: a group marked by majestic dignity or grandeur

venerable: old and respected; valued and respected because of old age, long use, etc.

Short Answer

1. He told them not to celebrate, but rather to let all of history celebrate for them.

2. He had not seen her in six years. He left all men and horses behind and walked on foot to see her, knowing that she didn't want to see him enter with a parade. They visited for some time, but she never made mention of his renown.

3. He calmed the men. Then he managed to get them to agree to a peaceful resolution, which he promised to take before Congress himself. He convinced Congress to not only pay the soldiers what was due to them, but to also pay them for another five years. This incident "gave a new proof of the kindness of his heart, soundness of his judgment, and purity of the love of his country."

4. He sent fifteen hundred men to quell these mutineers, and contrasted their deplorable behavior to the veterans who had endured nakedness, hunger, and cold.

5. He said nothing more than this: "Remember, young man, never in the future to make a promise, even of a trivial kind, the nature and extent of which you have not duly considered; having made it, let nothing prevent a punctual performance of it, if it be within your power."

6. Every entry was made by his own hand, and it was easy to find the corresponding receipts. His honesty was clearly seen in this matter.

7. He worked on his farm, constantly welcoming guests who stopped in to express their gratitude for his service. He also contributed to efforts to make rivers more navigable in order to stimulate economic progress in the country.

8. The French threw off moral restraints in an effort to achieve their freedom, and as such have been "unhappy" ever since.

9. You should enjoy the great blessing of freedom from unjust and oppressive laws, but you should beware of resisting the righteous laws of God. Freedom is not a license to sin, but an opportunity to worship the Creator.

Worksheet 7 Answer Key:

Vocabulary

dissolution: the process of making something slowly end or disappear

concourse: a meeting produced by voluntary or spontaneous coming together

tranquility: the quality or state of being at peace

homage: respect, honor

conspicuous: very easy to see or notice

meritorious: deserving of honor or esteem

unremitted: continuously maintained; uninterrupted

privateer: an armed private ship licensed to attack enemy shipping

insolent: rude or impolite; having or showing a lack of respect for other people

Short Answer

1. In sum, he argued that the nation had been dependent upon God during the war, but had somehow become dependent upon man in time of peace. Furthermore, he stated that without God, they would succeed no better than "the builders of Babel."

2. He was hesitant to serve, arguing that he lacked the political skills necessary. He humbly submitted to the will of the people, promising only "integrity and firmness."

3. A person can say they are going to do many things, but a close inspection of what they have done is a much better indication of what they'll do in the future. Answers will vary on part two.

4. He was always "punctual to the moment," not wishing to waste anyone's time.

5. There was war between France and England. Washington wanted the United States to stay neutral. He knew that the nation couldn't afford to be drawn into another war.

6. Congress had passed a tax on whiskey, and a number of backwoods farmers were committing violent acts in protest. Washington quickly organized a large group of troops to be sent out and quell the rebellion. They did so without bloodshed.

7. It is a "tyrant which chains the body in disgrace and poverty," and it "weakens the mind, and either destroys all recollection of the laws of God, or else causes a total disregard for them, and prepares the soul for everlasting punishment." Answers will vary on part two, but should be verses that warn of the dangers of strong drink.

8. Answers will vary, but should discuss the mutual respect between the two.

Worksheet 8 Answer Key:

Vocabulary

idleness: an inclination not to do work or engage in activities

dispositions: the attitudes or moods of a person

indigent: suffering from extreme poverty

frank: a signature or mark affixed by special privilege to a letter, package, or the like to ensure its transmission free of charge, as by mail.

trifling: of little importance; trivial

benefactor: one that confers a benefit; especially one that makes a gift

inculcated: implanted by repeated statement or admonition; taught persistently and earnestly

abhorrence: a feeling of disgust

proffered: put before a person for acceptance; offered

solicitude: concern that someone feels about someone's health, happiness, etc.

Short Answer

1. He would rise early, ride around the farm and conduct any necessary business there. He also had a habit of daily prayers, and vigorously kept the Sabbath.

2. Religion and morality are "indispensable supports" for political prosperity.

3. Answers could include (but aren't limited to): he paid for education for the poor, he kept a portion of his wheat to give to the needy, and he even let an old attendant of General Braddock live on his farm for the rest of his life.

4. The French had failed to negotiate in good faith with American envoys sent there to preserve peace. Our nation neared war with the French.

5. Washington went out into the cold to review his farm. He developed a severe cold. The doctors tried various primitive treatments including bleeding at least three times. He finally succumbed on December 14, 1799.

6. Answers will vary. There is much evidence to the contrary. A great deal of Washington's public statements show a clear respect for God and view Him as an active force in the world. The conclusion includes the testimony of household servants and relatives who observed Washington's private prayer and devotional life.

7. Answers will vary, but should include specific reasons as to why Washington is worthy of our imitation. Topics that could be addressed include his wisdom, leadership, honesty, control of passions, universal respect, strong faith in God, etc.

Life of Andrew Jackson — Worksheet Answer Keys

Worksheet 9 Answer Key:

Vocabulary

incipient: beginning to develop or exist

surplice: a loose, white piece of clothing that is worn by priests

habiliments: the dress characteristic of an occupation or occasion; clothing

imbrued: stained

sallying: suddenly attacking by rushing forward against an enemy

dragoons: a member of a European military unit composed of heavily armed mounted troops

execration: the act of cursing or denouncing

assuage: to make (something, such as an unpleasant feeling) less painful, severe, etc.

redoubt: a small usually temporary enclosed defensive work

patrimony: an estate inherited from one's father or ancestor

desultory: not connected with the main subject

Short Answer

1. The book was written as an attempt to give a full and complete account of the early life of Jackson, as well as give a more impartial account of his character.

2. Political parties had become more organized and polarized. The author seems to infer that Jackson was not being given a fair assessment at that time in history (only 13 years after he left the presidency, and only five years since his death).

3. Many people loved Jackson and many others hated him. But whatever the case, you couldn't ignore him. He was a bold person who provoked bold feelings.

4. Answers will vary, but should probably include a discussion of the importance of his relationship to his mother. It also required him to mature into a man at a very young age.

5. His family had fought British tyranny and oppression. His mother told her boys the stories of that struggle. (Jackson's grandfather had taken part in the siege of Carrickfergus.) As a result, their family sympathized with the American cause, as it was comparable to the Scottish struggle.

6. Answers will vary, but it probably caused him to be a soldier and it likely contributed to the violent life he lived as a young man. It also contributed to the fearlessness he would show his whole life, both in battle and in politics.

7. Jackson was taken prisoner by the British. He refused to clean a soldier's boots, stating that he should be treated with the respect a prisoner of war is due. The soldier struck at the young Jackson's head with his sword, but the blow was deflected by Jackson's left hand.

8. He began to gamble and drink, and blew his entire inheritance, except for his horse.

9. Like the prodigal son, he left home and wasted his inheritance on riotous living. Unlike the prodigal, he had no family to return to. He did, however, settle down and start studying law.

10. Answers will vary, but should include a discussion of his mother's role, his loss of all his family, and his participation in the Revolutionary War.

Worksheet 10 Answer Key:

Vocabulary

cataract: waterfall

circuitous: not straight, short, or direct

churlishness: impoliteness; vulgarity

bivouac: to make a temporary camp with little or no shelter

writ: an official, written court order

provocation: an action or occurrence that causes someone to become angry

depredation: laying waste to; plundering

appellation: an identifying name or title

morose: very serious, unhappy, and quiet; gloomy

affability: friendliness

expostulate: to disagree with something or argue against it

posse comitatus: the body of persons that a peace officer of a county is empowered to call upon for assistance in preserving the peace, making arrests, and serving writs.

dirk: a long, straight-bladed dagger

remonstrate: to disagree and argue or complain about something

inimical: being adverse often by reason of hostility; not friendly

Short Answer

1. He was exposed to many dangers, but never seemed to flinch. He developed strong leadership skills, often leading groups of people through this untamed wilderness. He also developed a reputation for being someone that shouldn't be provoked to anger.

2. U.S. Attorney for the new Tennessee judicial district; delegate to the Tennessee state constitutional convention; member of the U.S. House of Representatives; U.S. Senator; judge on the Tennessee Supreme Court

3. Jackson would not back down. In one instance he hit a man with a slab; in another he charged a man with his cane as if he were an ancient knight. Jackson was quickly moved to anger, and he would act upon it.

4. It was given to him by Native Americans as a nod to his courage and gallantry.

5. When he first moved to Tennessee, he boarded with her family. She was married to a Mr. Robards, but that marriage was rocky and eventually ended in divorce. In fact, Jackson's association with this woman was used as grounds for a divorce to be finalized. Jackson married her before the divorce was formalized in Virginia.

6. He was known to be a firm but fair judge.

7. Jackson's life teaches that this fidelity to friends can lead a person into disputes where he doesn't belong. Also, it can cause a person to be blind to the faults of friends, and leave them defending someone who is in the wrong.

8. Answers will vary, but it likely has to do with his weak educational background. It might also have something to do with his temper.

Worksheet 11 Answer Key:

Vocabulary

officious: volunteering one's services where they are neither asked nor needed; meddlesome

promptitude: the quality or habit of being punctual

reconnoitre: to go to (a place or area) in order to find out information about a military enemy

privations: a lack or loss of the basic things that people need to live properly

presages: something that foreshadows or portends a future event; omens

censure: an official act of reprimand or condemnation

caucus: a group of people who meet to discuss a particular issue

calamitous: causing great harm or suffering

torpor: a state of not being active and having very little energy

Short Answer

1. There was a dispute between the two over a horse-racing incident. Insults and letters were exchanged over a period of days until Jackson challenged him to duel on May 23. This incident reveals several insights into the nature of Andrew Jackson: he was fiercely loyal, he was chivalrous to a fault, he had no fear of anyone or death itself, and he was given to hotheadedness.

2. Jackson promptly sold his plantation, paid his debts, and moved into a log cabin. He quickly was able to recover, however.

3. In Jackson's own words, "I always carry mine with me: I am a free-born American citizen; and that is a passport all over the world."

4. Answers will vary, but it's likely that Jackson would recoil at many of our government's intrusions into personal liberty.

5. Answers will vary. It could imply that he was able to move past these sorts of incidents, or maybe he was just politically astute.

6. He was roused by the insults repeatedly offered to his country and by the bitter recollections connected with the death of his mother and two brothers. And don't forget, he had a scar on his hand to constantly remind himself of the atrocities of the British.

7. His men had marched from Nashville to Natchez, Mississippi, in the winter. Many were sick. He refused to let them go or enlist in the regular army because he felt a duty to return these young men home safely. And that's what he did.

8. Answers will vary, but should focus on Jackson's personal characteristics.

Worksheet 12 Answer Key:

Vocabulary

imperious: intensely compelling; urgent

forbearance: the quality of someone who is patient and able to deal with a difficult person or situation without becoming angry

ardor: energy, enthusiasm, or passion

bane: a source of harm or ruin

accoutrements: accessory items of clothing or equipment

lassitude: the condition of being tired; lack of physical or mental energy

consternation: a strong feeling of surprise or sudden disappointment that causes confusion

trepidation: a feeling of fear that causes you to hesitate

discomfiture: defeat in battle

indemnified: to make compensation to for incurred hurt, loss, or damage

Short Answer

1. Answers will vary, but should consider the effects of the time period in which the book was written.

2. Jackson imposed a strict attention to discipline among his men. He was particularly focused on orderliness, promptness, and limiting alcoholic beverages in his camp. He believed that soldiers disciplined in camp would fight in an effective and orderly manner when hostilities erupted.

3. He had trouble obtaining supplies and provisions for his men. He improvised all along the way in order to feed his troops.

4. He charged them to be disciplined, decisive, orderly, and brave. Moreover, he pleaded that as they fought they should be "mindful of what is due to humanity."

5. Jackson adopted him and raised him as his own son. Some say this incident proves that Jackson wasn't just a heartless killer of Indians; others say it was done just to soften his image. In either case, it surely proves that Jackson was a complex person. This complexity is largely why historians are so divided on his merits.

6. The Hermitage

Worksheet 13 Answer Key:

Vocabulary

amicable: characterized by friendly goodwill; peaceable

rivulet: a small stream of water

offal: the organs (such as the liver or kidney) of an animal that are used for food

repast: a meal

tripe: the stomach of an animal that is eaten as food

wo-begone: looking or feeling very sad

chagrined: frustrated or annoyed because of failure or disappointment

sumptuous: extremely costly, rich, luxurious, or magnificent

auspiciously: showing or suggesting that future success is likely

satiety: a feeling or condition of being full after eating food

expatiate: to speak or write about something in great detail

Short Answer

1. Jackson purchased supplies with his own money.

2. Like Washington, Jackson also provided for others without the recipient knowing the source.

3. Jackson shared his pocket full of acorns. The soldier returned to his fellow soldiers and told them that they should stop complaining.

4. He played the volunteers against the militia; he pleaded with the men; he bought time with the little provisions he was able to acquire; and ultimately he threatened to kill them all or die trying.
5. Answers can vary greatly on this set of questions.

Worksheet 14 Answer Key:

Vocabulary

intrepidity: strength of mind to carry on in spite of danger

defile: a narrow passage through mountains

grape shot: a cluster of small cast-iron balls formerly used as a charge for a cannon.

incantation: a use of spells or verbal charms spoken or sung as a part of a ritual of magic

disinterred: took (a body) out of a grave or tomb

flambeaux: a flaming torch

husbandry: the cultivation or production of plants or animals

prevaricate: to avoid telling the truth by not directly answering a question

impunity: exemption or freedom from punishment, harm, or loss

Short Answer

1. Jackson sent him to his own house in Tennessee and got him started in business when the war ended.
2. "He is a man who intends when he gives an order that it shall be obeyed," replied Gordon. Milton decided that he would, on second thought, give the assistance that Jackson requested.
3. Answers will vary, but should be sure to show the complexity of his character.
4. It called on the people of the southern territories to throw off the United States government and join with the British to fight for the soil that was rightfully theirs. It told them to not fear the Indians that they had recruited into their cause.
5. Answers will vary, but must give evidence in support.

Worksheet 15 Answer Key:

Vocabulary

formidable: very powerful or strong; very difficult to deal with

feint: a mock blow or attack on or toward one part in order to distract attention from the point one really intends to attack

evinced: clearly showed

concerted: done in a planned and deliberate way usually by several or many people

yeomanry: a group made up of common, small farmers

sally: a sudden attack in which a group of soldiers rush forward

temerity: unreasonable or foolhardy contempt of danger or opposition

impervious: not allowing entrance or passage; impenetrable

alacrity: a quick and cheerful readiness to do something

Short Answer

1. Martial law is the law administered by military forces that is invoked by a government in an emergency when the civilian law enforcement agencies are unable to maintain public order and safety. Jackson put New Orleans under martial law because he believed that there were too many subversive individuals in the city to keep it safe during the course of anticipated attack. Most of the settlers there were Spanish or French and may not have had too much patriotism toward the United States.
2. He had an officer translate to French the following statement: "Do not be alarmed. The enemy shall never reach the city!" His confidence operated "like an electric shock," and the city was filled with the confidence of this general.
3. The American success could be attributed to several factors: excellent planning by Jackson, valiant fighting, difficult terrain, the British perception that there would be little resistance, and perhaps most significantly, the darkness and fog in the night kept the British forces

from knowing that the Americans were without bayonets.

4. Jackson believed that since the British had vastly superior numbers, that another attack in daylight could prove fatal to the Americans. Moreover, he found it more important that the city of New Orleans be protected and not fall into the hands of the opposition.

5. Jackson had less than 2,000 men. The British had between 4,000 and 5,000.

Worksheet 16 Answer Key:

Vocabulary

sagacity: having or showing an ability to understand difficult ideas and situations and to make good decisions

judicious: having or showing good judgment

exigencies: that which is required in a particular situation

overweening: too great; excessive and unpleasant; exaggerated

conjecture: an opinion or idea formed without proof or sufficient evidence

embrasures: openings with sides flaring outward in a wall to allow the firing of cannons

videttes: mounted sentinels stationed in advance of pickets

scruple: to show reluctance on grounds of conscience; hesitate

assiduity: diligence

palliate: to cover by excuses and apologies

nefarious: flagrantly wicked or impious

ambuscade: ambush

Short Answer

1. Clear-headed sagacity, promptness of decision, and rapidity of execution.

2. Our enemy can attack us at unexpected times and in circumstances beyond our control. Our best offense is to build our spiritual defenses in advance.

3. He didn't sleep! He was too busy personally overseeing the fortification of New Orleans.

4. He had the men cut the levee. This flooded the area below, making it nearly impassable.

5. Good men are a greater guarantee for success than any fortification one could build with hands.

6. Later that night in their quarters, they spoke loudly about the situation and inflated the number of men. They assumed they were being listened to and Shields was thought to be somewhat deaf, so it was a believable stunt.

7. He was going to burn the city. "I would have destroyed New Orleans — occupied a position above on the river — cut off all supplies, and in this way compelled them to depart from the country."

8. Jackson handed him a gun and ordered him to the front line, assuming that a man who possessed property had as much motivation to fight as anyone.

Worksheet 17 Answer Key:

Vocabulary

incessant: continuing without stopping; not stopping

precipitately: quickly or suddenly

abatement: becoming weaker; decreasing in strength

impetuosity: marked by force and violence of movement or action

galled: vexed or irritated greatly

licentious: sexually immoral or offensive

cupidity: strong desire; lust

debase: to lower the value or reputation of (someone or something)

enmity: a very deep unfriendly feeling

dastardly: very cruel or cowardly; characterized by treachery

gibbet: the gallows

glacis: a slope that runs downward from a fortification

Short Answer

1. The majority of them had no weapons. He placed them in the rear of the entrenchment to conceal their actual condition and hopefully give the appearance of added strength.

2. An American deserter alerted the British General that this area was defended by the militia, and the assumption was that these poorly trained soldiers would not be able to hold up against a concentrated assault.

3. He was implying that Jackson set a personal example of diligence, and his constant presence imbued the men with confidence.

4. The American soldiers cared for the wounded and dead British soldiers and were full of "charity and kindness." The British soldiers were motivated by "beauty and booty," and even fired upon American soldiers who were caring for the wounded and dying British soldiers.

5. The most significant factor was that Jackson had carefully selected the battlefield and built entrenchments that were very difficult to assault. He, of course, gave the credit to the valiant men who served under his command.

6. Answers will vary, but should focus on the example that Jackson set.

7. "Bold without being rash, daring without being reckless, his own noble bearing was sufficient to arouse emotions of patriotism where none had existed."

8. It leaves out significant details as to their unceremonious defeat.

Worksheet 18 Answer Key:

Vocabulary

encomium: glowing and warmly enthusiastic praise

rapine: pillage or plunder

fortitude: strength of mind that enables a person to encounter danger or bear pain or adversity with courage

pomp: a show of magnificence

incendiaries: verified or proven to be true in pleading a cause

parleying: discussing with an enemy or someone you disagree with, especially in order to end a conflict

writ of habeas corpus: a court order that requires a person under arrest to be brought to court

extricate: to free or remove from an entanglement or difficulty

Short Answer

1. They hailed him as their deliverer and protector.

2. Judge Hall tried to interfere with Jackson's arrest of one of the members of the legislature who had written a letter in a newspaper attempting to incite the troops to mutiny.

3. It was signed on December 24. Due to slow communication, word had not yet reached New Orleans. Thus, the Battle of New Orleans was actually fought after the war had officially concluded.

4. Jackson supporters filled the streets and quickly raised the fine to pay on his behalf. Jackson refused the money and paid the fine himself. The money raised for his support was given to a charitable institution at his request.

5. This text indicates that it is an allusion to his successful raids in the sacred Indian "Hickory Ground."

6. He was made the territorial governor of Florida, recently acquired from the Spanish.

7. Answers will vary, but should give specific evidence.

Worksheet 19 Answer Key:

Vocabulary

plenipotentiary: invested with full power

partisans: firm adherents to a party, faction, cause, or person

bereavement: the state of being sad because a family member or friend has recently died

irreparable: too bad to be corrected or repaired

averred: verified or proven to be true in pleading a cause

aloof: not involved in or influenced by something

parlance: language used by a particular group of people

temerity: unreasonable or foolhardy contempt of danger or opposition

asperity: harshness of behavior or speech that expresses bitterness or anger

chivalric: a way of acting or speaking in an honorable and polite way

Short Answer

1. The hardships of the Indian wars are given as the main cause, though his penchant for dueling in his younger days likely contributed as well.

2. Jackson received more electoral votes than any of the other candidates, but the House of Representatives chose John Quincy Adams instead. Speaker of the House Henry Clay was then chosen to be Secretary of State for Adams. Many believe that this arrangement was made in order to get the House to pick Adams over Jackson.

3. He was attacked for the circumstances surrounding his marriage, his conduct toward the Creek Indians, his attack on Pensacola, his arrest of Judge Hall, among several others.

4. He never really got over his bereavement. He even blamed the partisan attacks on her character as a contributing factor to her death.

5. The statement is in reference to his firmness in refusing to renew the charter of the national bank. The implication is that once Jackson made up his mind, he was not one to be moved.

6. Answers will vary, but hopefully will acknowledge that while being a good trait, a leader ought to still be able to adjust his or her opinion once proven wrong.

7. He was enormously popular even though he made many controversial moves.

8. In typical Jackson fashion, he stated that if he had known the man's intentions when he came in the room, he could assure you "that he would never again have the temerity to undertake such a thing."

9. The public debt has almost continually increased, particularly since the 1930s. Do an Internet search to find the most current figures, since they are so rapidly increasing.

Worksheet 20 Answer Key:

Vocabulary

dropsy: an abnormal infiltration and excess accumulation of serous fluid in connective tissue or in a serous **cavity**; edema

swooned: suddenly became unconscious

rancorous: marked by angry feelings of hatred or dislike for someone who has treated you unfairly

bedew: to wet with or as if with dew

intuitive: having the ability to know or understand things without any proof or evidence

celerity: rapidity of motion or action

groveling: giving oneself over to what is base or unworthy

Short Answer

1. They passed a law to reimburse Jackson for the $1,000 fine he paid at New Orleans, with interest included.

2. "In the hands of a merciful God, I have full confidence. . . . I am ready to depart when called. The Bible is true. . . . Upon that sacred volume I rest my hope of eternal salvation, through the merits and blood of our blessed Lord and Savior, Jesus Christ."

3. Answers will vary.

4. He said that he may have disagreed with the vast majority of Jackson's decisions as president, but he never doubted Jackson's patriotism or love of country. He also recognized the power of Jackson's influence and popularity.

5. He was prompt and resolute in battle; his courage and fortitude were unmatched; his readiness to adapt and succeed in any situation; he never forgot a favor or failed to remember a friend.

6. Answers will vary.

Worksheets 21 and 22 Answer Key:

Answers will vary, based upon the reading the student chooses. Assign credit as you see fit.

Life of Luther — Worksheet Answer Keys

Worksheet 23 Answer Key:

Vocabulary

edifice: a building, usually large and impressive

declivity: a downward slope

penury: extreme poverty

obstinacy: stubbornness

gamboling: running or jumping in a lively way

turbid: cloudy or muddy

credulous: ready to believe especially on slight or uncertain evidence

knaves: dishonest men

cogitations: thoughts or careful reflections

drollery: something odd or amusing

sottish: drunken

Short Answer

1. Luther's father is described as a sensible and honest man. He was open-hearted and frank, and was fearless of the consequences of following his judgment. He was firm to the point of obstinacy. His son would have many of these same characteristics that would serve him well in his efforts to reform as he was willing to face the harshest of opposition. His father encouraged him in his efforts, and even advised him to break the vow of celibacy.

2. She was pious, but much more religiously superstitious than his father. Her influence is one of the greatest reasons Luther chose to become a monk in the first place.

3. To trace out the causes that operated in the formation of Luther's character

4. Answers will vary, but the text suggests that Luther's harshness and violent streak was a result of the severe punishments he faced as a child.

5. It is a rather scathing critique: "a religion of law rather than of gospel; a Pelagian system of works rather than of divine grace . . . a religion of the senses and of a poetical imagination rather than of saving faith . . . a religion founded more on the ignorance and superstition of the middle ages than on the revelation of the truth by Jesus Christ and his apostles." (See page 35.)

6. Although the German Catholics were superstitious like the Italians, they were generally more sincere and earnest in their faith (much like Luther's mother).

7. "He was not a man of policy or calculation, but a true-hearted, conscientious man, a man of principle, whose great power consisted in doing right without regard to consequences."

8. As a result of his religious education, Luther viewed Christ as a "rigorous judge," who would deal with him according to his merits and works

9. He was able to connect well with the greatest mass of people. His homely manner of speaking and writing served him with a great advantage. In addition, he came from a part of Germany that was "the most German" of all the districts, as it belonged to no other section.

Worksheet 24 Answer Key:

Vocabulary

mendicant: someone (such as a member of a religious group) who lives by asking people for money or food

scapularies: garments consisting of a long, wide piece of woolen cloth worn over the shoulders with an opening for the head; part of a monastic habit

cowl: a hood or long, hooded cloak, especially of a monk

trifling: having little value or importance; trivial

pensive: quietly sad or thoughtful

indelibly: impossible to remove or forget; lasting or unforgettable

chagrin: a feeling of being frustrated or annoyed because of failure or disappointment

capacious: able to hold or contain a lot; large in capacity

prolix: marked by or using an excess of words

cloister: a place where monks or nuns live; a monastery or convent

propound: to suggest (an idea, theory, etc.) to a person or group of people to consider

Short Answer

1. He "procured his bread by choral and other services in the church." In effect, he was a beggar much of the time, as was the custom.

2. The painting showed a ship full of priests and monks with only laymen drowning in the water. This painting summarized their doctrine, and Luther later stated, "I was once one of them, and helped teach such things, believing them and knowing no better."

3. She showed him another side of life; that not all pleasures were evil, particularly the married life. This, of course, would be a significant influence on his decision to marry later in life.

4. He no longer had to beg for food and was able to focus more on his academic development. He was able to delve into classical literature, Aristotelian logic, etc. He took on a more cheery view of life.

5. He told Luther that he wouldn't die and that God was going to make a great man out of him.

6. Luther stumbled across a Bible while looking through other books. He marveled because the Bible contained much more than the postils circulated in the churches. He quickly devoured the story of Hannah and Samuel, and he began to wish for the day that he would have a Bible of his own.

7. Answers will vary, but the Word of God was kept from the masses of people.

Worksheet 25 Answer Key:

Vocabulary

propagate: to make (something, such as an idea or belief) known to many people

novitiate: the time when a person is a religious novice

languor: weakness or weariness of body or mind

antiphonies: responsive alternation between two groups, especially of singers

genuflection: the act of bowing on a knee in worship or awe

collation: a light meal allowed on fast days in place of lunch or supper

acquiescence: accepting, agreeing, or allowing something to happen by staying silent or by not arguing

vitiated: made less effective; ruined or spoiled

mote: speck; small particle

demure: quiet, modest, and polite

colloquy: conversation, dialogue

Short Answer

1. It was at the cloister at Erfurt that Luther first began his conversion from the Catholic faith as a result of his studies and his slow realization that salvation was not possible through his good works.

2. Justification by faith alone, and private judgment in interpreting Scripture

3. In his view, this pious life would be the surest way of pleasing God.

4. He was nearly struck by lightning, and in his terror made this rash vow.

5. Luther's father didn't want him to go, and argued the biblical command that children should obey their parents. The monks focused on Scriptures that proscribe hesitancy in the Kingdom of God. ("Whosoever putteth his hand to the plough and looketh back is not worthy of the kingdom of God.") Answers will vary on the opinion portion of the question.

6. Had Luther not spent those formative years as a monk, he may not have seen just how corrupt the church had become, and then may not have initiated the immense changes brought on by the Reformation.

7. Answers will vary, but should focus on the rigorous personal discipline required. Also, it should be noted that the other monks didn't care much for Luther's love for studying.

8. No matter how carefully he confessed, he always doubted the completeness of his confession. This left him in a constant state of weariness because of his view that God was an angry judge, ready to prosecute.

9. The Bible was not studied as a whole, but in small pieces removed from context. The author could not be his own interpreter. The literal sense was "deserted at pleasure, and an allegorical one introduced to suit the object of the interpreter."

10. Answers will vary, but should focus on his experience as a novice monk.

Worksheet 26 Answer Key:

Vocabulary

efficacious: having the power to produce a desired result or effect

mien: a person's appearance or facial expression

benighted: existing in a state of intellectual, moral, or social darkness; unenlightened

labyrinth: something that is extremely complicated or difficult to understand

disquisition: a formal inquiry into or discussion of a subject; discourse

execrable: very bad; wretched

ablution: the washing of one's body or part of it (as in a religious rite)

lucre: monetary gain; profit

parricide: a murder of one's father, mother, or a close relative

raillery: good-natured ridicule; banter

adduce: to offer as example, reason, or proof in discussion or analysis

cumbrous: hard to manage or handle

Short Answer

1. Once Luther purposed to do something, he wasn't someone to quit. It seems he made up his mind from the beginning.

2. Staupitz actually encouraged Luther to study the Scripture. He also nurtured many of the spiritual questions Luther was beginning to have. He was one of the primary instigators of Luther's conversion to evangelicalism.

3. A priest was to be a mediator between God and man. Luther was so conscious of his sinfulness that he was terrified to hold such an exalted position.

4. He felt it obscured Christ.

5. Catholic: God is foremost a judge to be feared; good works are sought as a recommendation to God.

   Protestant: God is a loving Savior who forgives gratuitously, meeting the sinner where he is and bearing his load.

6. Righteousness had meant that God is just and punishes the guilty. But upon closer study of Paul's writings, particularly Romans 1:19, he came to understand that God's righteousness is revealed in His mercy and compassion.

Worksheet 27 Answer Key:

Vocabulary

refectory: a large room where meals are served

luminous: clear, enlightening

exculpate: to prove that someone is not guilty of doing something wrong

vehement: intensely emotional; impassioned, fervid

Short Answer

1. Because Luther was so modest and reluctant, Staupitz initially had him go to the monastery at Wittenberg and lecture there on philosophy.

2. Contrary to the usual custom, it was under the protection of the elector, and not of the pope, or a cardinal, or an archbishop.

3. There had recently been a problem with intoxication and the open wielding of guns. The religious atmosphere was consumed with superstition, particularly an obsession with relics and indulgences.

4. He never received anything from his students for his labors or from booksellers for his writings.

5. He said, "When I go up into the pulpit, I do not look upon any one. I think them to be only so many blocks before me, and I speak out the words of my God." Answers will vary on part two.

6. Luther had taken an oath to teach purely and sincerely to the Scriptures. Catholic leaders supposed there was a substantial agreement between the teachings of the church and those

of the Bible. Once Luther came under the conviction that the church's teachings were not biblical, he then used the oath he had taken as justification for his agitation.

7. The only Bible he had at his disposal was the Latin Vulgate, which in his estimation was full of errors.

8. Much of the timidity and submissiveness that he had been known for had eroded, and the tone of his letters became decidedly more authoritative — a trait that would come to define him during the Reformation.

Worksheet 28 Answer Key:

Vocabulary

disputatious: inclined to dispute; provoking debate

maledictions: curses; execrations

pernicious: causing great harm or damage, often in a way that is not easily seen or noticed

ignominiously: marked with or characterized by disgrace or shame; dishonorably

decorous: correct and polite in a particular situation

erudite: having or showing knowledge that is learned by studying

obstreperous: stubbornly resistant to control; unruly

Short Answer

1. He will begin to take a position of great publicity. For the historian, this is especially crucial because from this point forward, Luther's life is very carefully chronicled.

2. Because Aristotle's teachings were put in the place of the prophets and apostles by theologians, and Luther found this to be perverse.

3. This time, there were "no traces of the shrinking timidity which he manifested in 1509, when he was appointed preacher, and in 1512, when he was made doctor of divinity." This suggests that a significant level of personal growth and leadership development occurred during the intervening years. One could also infer that he was preparing to make a public defense of his new views, and this position of leadership could be a significant springboard for it.

4. Answers will vary, but a summary should include basic ideas such as these — Social: he had reluctantly taken positions of leadership, but that reluctance began to fall away, and a new-found boldness is seen in his letters. Intellectual: he had begun to attack much of the philosophical teachings in the university and the church. Theological: he had fully adopted the concept of salvation by faith alone, and began to openly attack the idea of a works-based faith.

Worksheet 29 Answer Key:

Vocabulary

contrariety: the quality or state of being contrary; incompatibleness

nominally: in a very small quantity or degree

plenary: complete in every respect; absolute, unqualified

sepulchre: a place of burial; a receptacle for religious relics, especially in an altar

legate: an official representative of the pope

itinerating: traveling from place to place to perform one's professional duty.

degeneracy: the state of declining moral standards

transient: not lasting long

Short Answer

1. In one, the agent was the church; in the other, the agent was Christ. In one, the sinner must be reformed by penances; in the other, he was to exercise godly sorrow for sin and faith in Christ. The one was external and sacramental; the other was internal and spiritual.

2. The priest had taken the role as mediator between God and man, lord of the individual conscience, and infallible judge. In essence, the priest had taken the role of Christ.

3. Contrition, confession, satisfaction

4. Luther had three major questions: How was one to know that his penitence was sufficient? How would he be sure that no individual sin was omitted in the confession? Why should absolution be pronounced before the conditions were all fulfilled, before satisfaction was known to be made?

5. In effect, indulgences had become a tax for sins.
6. Tetzel was a greedy, self-righteous person. He placed himself above Peter and even Christ, and shamefully sold indulgences for his own profit.
7. John of Goch, John of Wesel, and John Wessel.

Worksheet 30 Answer Key:

Vocabulary

decalogue: a basic set of rules carrying binding authority

servile: very obedient and trying too hard to please someone

abstruse: hard to understand

confuted: overwhelmed in argument; refuted conclusively

impugn: to criticize by suggesting that someone is not honest and should not to be trusted

superlatively: of the highest kind, quality, or order; surpassing all else or others

supercilious: coolly and patronizingly haughty

inveighed: protested or bitterly complained

fulminate: to complain loudly or angrily

odium: disrepute or infamy attached to something; opprobrium

corpulent: fat

magnanimity: loftiness of spirit enabling one to bear trouble calmly, to disdain meanness and pettiness, and to display a noble generosity

Short Answer

1. He would rather people give their money to the poor, because there was a clear biblical basis for it, while the biblical basis for indulgences was questionable in his eyes. Moreover, he saw grace as a free gift of God, which made indulgences unnecessary.
2. He refused to administer the supper, unless they first made confession. This was because he felt that repentance was being overlooked in this whole process, and without repentance, none of the other religious trappings really mattered.
3. He had requested that his superiors intervene into this evil activity, but they refused to act, and some disregarded his letters completely. His 95 theses were designed to open a dialogue between the theological minds of his community.
4. The 95 theses were not written for an audience of laymen. They were "ill adapted for the common people." But once they had been taken and published by his friends, he found it necessary to write a more colloquial version for the general public.
5. Luther faced much opposition, but did manage a few converts among the younger generations. Numerous papers were published against him, and public disputations were held.

Worksheet 31 Answer Key:

Vocabulary

parsimonious: frugal to the point of stinginess

puerile: childish, juvenile, or silly

decretals: decrees

dogmas: a set of beliefs that is taught by a religious organization

prefatory: included at the beginning of a book, speech, etc., as an introduction

enigmatically: mysteriously

requital: something given in return, compensation, or retaliation

promulgated: made known to many people

sordid: very bad or dishonest

Short Answer

1. It explains his view of the centrality of repentance, which came about as a result of his study of the Bible in the original languages. It also explains how and why he was taking on such a public role in the debate.
2. The letter carefully explains how Luther had not intended the 95 Theses for public consumption and how the whole debate had spun out of his control quickly. It is most important, historically, because it shows Luther's views of Leo and the papacy in general at this time. You see that Luther is still loyal to the authority of the pope at this point: "I will acknowledge your voice as the voice of Christ presiding and speaking in you."

3. He began writing letters to influential friends, seeking to avoid having to travel to Rome. He felt like he was being set up.
4. Melancthon, who was brought to the university to teach Greek
5. Answers will vary, but the evidence shows that even into late 1518, although he was subversive to the church leaders, he was still willing to submit to their questions . . . if they would ever give them to him.

Worksheet 32 Answer Key:

Vocabulary

paternoster: a word formula repeated as a prayer or magical charm

unapt: inappropriate, unsuitable, or unlikely

nuncio: a person who is the pope's representative in a foreign country

peradventure: perhaps; possibly

hellebore: a poisonous herb, once used for medicinal purposes

potentates: powerful rulers

plenitude: a large number or amount of something

Short Answer

1. Answers will vary.
2. The denial that the merits and sufferings of Christ are the treasure of the church, and the assertion that faith was necessary in order to partake of the Holy Communion. Luther agreed to recant if his assertions were indeed proven incorrect, but since they couldn't be, he refused to recant.
3. "A clear proof that Rome hath more care for money than for faith and salvation."
4. First, he agreed to drop the matter if his adversaries would do the same. Second, he agreed to write the pope, submit humbly to him, and to admit that he'd been too heated and violent. Third, he agreed to set forth an address exhorting all to follow the Roman church, and to interpret his writings in a way to bring honor upon the church.
5. Answers will vary, but should have specific examples of weaknesses.

Worksheet 33 Answer Key:

Vocabulary

disingenuous: not truly honest or sincere; giving the false appearance of being honest or sincere

sycophancy: self-seeking flattery

contumely: harsh language or treatment arising from haughtiness and contempt

suborned: persuaded (someone) to do something illegal (such as to lie in a court of law)

perfidious: not able to be trusted; showing that someone cannot be trusted

chasuble: a sleeveless outer vestment worn by the officiating priest at mass

garrulity: pointlessly or annoyingly talkative

gesticulation: the act of making expressive gestures

polemic: a strong written or spoken attack against someone else's opinions, beliefs, etc.

adroitness: very clever or skillful

perdition: utter destruction; eternal damnation

spurious: not genuine, sincere, or authentic

Short Answer

1. Eck, Carlstadt, and Luther
2. Eck carefully drew Luther into the debate by publicly attacking Luther's theology. Luther had agreed to drop matters if his opponents did the same. Eck's calculated ploy to get Luther into the debate was successful.
3. Luther, in letters to the pope and others, still claimed his allegiance to Rome and only asked to be left to the "pure gospel." Yet he continued to argue against the power of the church and the pope in particular. The author states that this is because "he was in reality the subject of an inward struggle between two contending forces, drawing him alternately in opposite directions."
4. Answers will vary, but should be focused on the Christian responsibility to honor authority.
5. It was useful for the cause of the Reformation in opening the eyes of Luther himself on the whole subject of papal authority, and in drawing public attention to the issue. It caused a few papists to join him, but it created even greater opposition

to his teachings among the others. Many of Luther's troubles that came in the next year or two were a direct result of this debate (Page 294).

6. Luther's commentary on the Epistle to the Galatians

Worksheet 34 Answer Key:

Vocabulary

escutcheon: a shield or emblem bearing a coat of arms.

iota: a very small amount

bespeaking: to speak to, especially with formality; address

preconcerted: previously arranged

exchequer: treasury

cavalcade: a procession of riders or carriages

Short Answer

1. The German princes had "long felt the galling yolk of Roman tyranny," and were tired of paying "enormous tribute" under various forms to the church.

2. Luther had already been condemned by the pope, and to bring him in for a secular tribunal would, in effect, undermine the power of the pope.

3. Luther fully expected to lose his life, much like Huss had. This shows the courage and resolve that Luther possessed, and it shows how much he believed in his theological findings.

4. They piled up his books on a table and asked, "Are these your books, and will you retract them or their contents?"

5. Luther admitted the books were his, but asked for more time to contemplate the second question. They gave him until the next day to answer.

6. He argued that his books were of three different classes. Some were clearly and simply harmless, and he couldn't renounce those. Some were directed against the pope and Rome, and if he were to revoke these, he would give strength to tyranny. The third class was directed against individuals. He admitted these to be too harsh in tone, but he would not be able to revoke these either.

7. "Unless I shall be convinced by the testimony of Scripture, or by clear and plain argument . . . I am held by those passages which I have cited, and am bound by my conscience and by the word of God, and therefore I may not — cannot retract, inasmuch as it is neither safe nor right to violate my conscience. Here I stand, and cannot do otherwise, God be my help. Amen."

8. Answers will vary.

Worksheet 35 Answer Key:

Vocabulary

costiveness: constipation

derision: the use of ridicule or scorn to show contempt

auricular: told privately

prelate: a high-ranking Christian priest; a bishop, cardinal, etc.

aspersion: a sprinkling with water especially in religious ceremonies

jocosely: cheerfully; jokingly

Short Answer

1. It gave him time for reflection (something he hadn't had time for in months, perhaps years).

2. During this period, it seems that religious liberty was almost "indispensable" to him, but later on he was less inclined than before to the freedom of conscience in the interpretation of the Bible.

3. He "felt his blood boil within him." He wrote a very pointed tract against the bishop, but his friends convinced him not to publish it. Instead he wrote a letter to the man directly.

4. They knew that his response was too bold for the circumstances and endeavored to calm him down and get him to think more clearly. It is essential for us to have friends who hold us accountable and keep us from pursuing a course that is not the wisest choice.

5. People everywhere began to exercise freedom of opinion and speech. Schisms developed over several questions: How is this freedom

to be controlled? Shall men be free to differ from Luther himself? Is there no subjection to authority in matters of religion? Shall the civil power be brought in as the protector of true faith?

6. Carlstadt insisted on bringing back the pattern of the primitive church in its entirety. He opposed all ceremonies introduced by the later church. Luther was somewhat indifferent on matters of outward conformity.

7. He was fearful that the whole movement would be discredited by the radicals and, as the spokesman of the movement, only he could stem the tide.

Worksheet 36 Answer Key:

Vocabulary

harangued: lectured; gave a speech to a large assembly

ribaldry: use of crude, indecent, or offensive speech

courtiers: members of a royal court

pertinacity: the quality of being persistent and tenacious

expostulation: disagreeing with something or arguing against it

dissimulation: deceiving someone with false information

inveterate: always or often happening or existing

grotesque: departing markedly from the natural, the expected, or the typical

Short Answer

1. They were not showing love in the way they were dealing with the situation.

2. Doing away with mass and destroying icons are two good examples. While Luther opposed these things, he felt that "no one should be forced to faith, but should be drawn to it and won by the word." He didn't think people should use their freedom to shock the feeling of other pious persons.

3. Pope Leo X died in 1521 and was replaced by Hadrian VI, who took a different direction in policy. Moreover, Charles V was embroiled in war with France, and was thus distracted.

4. Answers will vary.

5. Carlstadt believed that Christians should only participate in activities clearly found in the Bible. Luther believed that Christians could participate in activities that were not explicitly found in Scripture, as long as they weren't explicitly forbidden by it. In addition, Carlstadt found the Law of Moses still binding, and Luther did not. Most importantly, they differed on the Lord's Supper — Carlstadt holding that people partook only in a "spiritual" sense, Luther opposing transubstantiation, but still supporting consubstantiation, the real presence, and the adoration of the host.

6. Transubstantiation: the belief that the bread and wine given at communion become the actual body and blood of Jesus Christ when they are blessed.

   Consubstantiation: the belief that the substance of the body and blood of Christ are present alongside the actual bread and wine.

7. They both "exceeded the bounds of Christian propriety and moderation."

8. Luther was very concerned about the Reformation being discredited by the mass political movements that sometimes resulted in fanaticism. As a result, he held to divine right of kings and the doctrine of passive obedience on the part of their subjects. He traveled about trying to quell the democratic fervor sweeping the masses.

Worksheet 37 Answer Key:

Vocabulary

fetters: chains or shackles; restraints

tattled: uttered or disclosed in gossip or chatter

amanuensis: one employed to write from dictation or to copy manuscript

conjugal: relating to marriage or to a married couple

circumlocution: the use of an unnecessarily large number of words to express an idea

avarice: excessive or insatiable desire for wealth or gain; greediness, cupidity

Short Answer

1. Luther had a man named Koppe do this. He lifted the women over the wall and put them into barrels in a wagon. When asked what was in his barrels, he replied, "Barrels of herring."
2. He figured his life to always be in jeopardy and hated to enter into matrimony only to leave behind a grieving wife.
3. He feared the marriage of a monk to a nun would, on account of a two-fold violation of the monastic vow, stir up the public and there would be attempts to prevent it from happening.
4. Answers will vary, but it appears that they had a happy marriage.
5. He was a poor manager of money. He was accustomed to living on very little from his days as a monk, and he was extraordinarily generous to the needy, so much so that he often found himself in debt. His wife was a much shrewder manager of funds.

Worksheet 38 Answer Key:

Vocabulary

castigate: to subject to severe punishment, reproof, or criticism

vivacity: lively or happily

amorous: having or showing strong feelings of sexual attraction or love

Short Answer

1. He was experienced — he preached every day and often multiple times. He preached in the native language, which was compelling for this time. His appearance helped — his manly form, his piercing eyes, and his penetrating voice. His intelligence, wit, quickness of memory, and poetic composition should be considered. Most importantly, he preached the gospel, and people were moved by its message and the conviction with which Luther communicated it.
2. If people were going to be their own interpreter of Scripture, they needed a solid education to undergird their studies.
3. He believed that parents had a biblical responsibility to educate their children.
4. Luther saw music as a beautiful and lovely gift of God. He thought it was second only to theology.
5. Answers will vary. Some positive qualities would include his brilliant mind, unswerving devotion, fearlessness, etc. Some negative qualities would include his combativeness, his tendency toward dispute and pettiness, his abrasive language, his frequent fits of melancholy, etc.

Life of John Knox — Worksheet Answer Keys

Worksheet 39 Answer Key:

Vocabulary

extirpate: to destroy completely; wipe out

declaimed: spoken pompously or bombastically; harangued

aversion: a feeling of repugnance toward something with a desire to avoid or turn from it

artifice: dishonest or insincere behavior or speech that is meant to deceive someone

retinue: a group of helpers, supporters, or followers

dowager: a widow holding property or a title from her deceased husband

expostulating: reasoning earnestly with a person for purposes of dissuasion or remonstrance

inconstancy: the frequent changing of one's mind without apparent reason

Short Answer

1. His burning zeal and unbending faithfulness
2. Jerome and Augustine
3. Answers will vary, but should note that the

landscape was constantly shifting. The Protestants would be treated well for a short time, and then face horrible persecution shortly thereafter.

4. After the murder of Wishart, a number of overzealous reformers decided to assassinate the cardinal at St. Andrews. Realizing the gravity of their actions, they decided to fortify their position, and many other Protestants took refuge there.

5. He was asked to become a public teacher, but he did not believe he had a proper call to that work.

6. Like Luther, Knox was also very hesitant to teach. Both felt a great weight of responsibility in holding such a high office.

7. He was a very eloquent defender of the Protestant doctrines, but was most known for how plainly he spoke against the Catholic faith (and particularly individuals in leadership).

8. Because he spoke so harshly against political leaders, he was constantly forced to leave the country for the sake of his own safety.

Worksheet 40 Answer Key:

Vocabulary

solicited: asked

dauphin: the eldest son of a king

effrontery: shameless boldness; insolence

precipitation: the quality or state of being precipitate; hastiness

detestation: extreme hatred or dislike; abhorrence, loathing

remonstrances: protests or complaints about something

reft: robbed or plundered

languid: showing or having very little strength, energy, or activity

indurate: physically or morally hardened

appertains: belongs to or is connected or related to something

Short Answer

1. Properly qualified persons should be able to read the Scriptures every Lord's day; the sacraments should be administered in the language of the people; preaching and the interpretation of Scripture should be private

2. Mill was burned for renouncing the errors of popery. He was held in high regard, so much so that the people would not provide ropes to bind him or materials for his execution. Once he was burned at St. Andrews, it gave "the death-blow to popery in Scotland."

3. A Catholic priest struck a young Protestant boy after the boy spoke against the idolatry of the mass.

4. He was told not to preach there, but he ignored these warnings stating that his life was "in the custody of Him whose glory I seek." He feared the calling on his life by God more than the queen's army.

5. Answers will vary.

6. "If I teach the truth of God in sincerity — if to rebuke idolatry, and to exhort the people to worship God according to his word, be to raise rebel lion, I am certainly liable to the charge. . . ."

7. There was much distrust between the two. She was queen, yet she feared Knox because of his popularity among a vast number in her country. Knox was emboldened by God, but also knew that Mary couldn't touch him without arousing serious consequences.

Worksheet 41 Answer Key:

Vocabulary

indefatigable: incapable of being fatigued; untiring

actuated: caused to do something or to act in a certain way

apoplectic: affected with, inclined to, or showing symptoms of stroke

contrivers: devisers; planners

abhor: extreme dislike; loathe

calamity: a disastrous event marked by great loss and lasting distress and suffering

traduced: exposed to shame or blame by means of falsehood and misrepresentation

austere: stern and cold in appearance or manner

thralldom: the state of being a slave

Short Answer

1. It serves to teach the biblical truth that you will reap what you sow.
2. A musket was fired through the window at the position where he normally sat. Providentially, Knox had changed his seat that evening, avoiding what likely would have been his death.
3. John 17 is Jesus' prayer for His disciples — the last before His arrest. As leader of the Scottish Reformation, Knox likely felt as though he was in a similar situation, with his death imminent. Isaiah 53 is the prophecy of the death of Jesus. Knox probably preferred to hear this Scripture in order to give comfort to his own situation.
4. He said that he never hated them, but hated their sin. "My impartiality in reproving men of every rank was dictated by the fear of God . . . who will call me into account."
5. "There lies he who never feared the face of man; who hath often been threatened with pistol and dagger; but yet hath ended his days in peace and honor; for Providence watched over him in a special manner, when his very life was in danger."
6. He says that these characteristics were "absolutely necessary" for constituting a reformer. If he had been gentler in spirit, he would have been unfit for the task that God had called him to. Answers will vary on part two.
7. The talents that are suited to one age and station would be altogether unsuitable to another, and we should keep in mind that what is needed for the furtherance of God's kingdom will be different from age to age.
8. John the Baptist
9. Answers will vary, but should focus on the boldness and outspoken manner which both men displayed throughout their lives.

Life of John Newton — Worksheet Answer Keys

Worksheet 42 Answer Key:

Vocabulary

propensities: strong natural tendencies to do something

protracted: delayed or deferred

contiguous: being in actual contact; touching along a boundary or at a point

pittance: a very small amount of money

caprices: sudden changes in mood or behavior

necromances: magic, sorcery

amulets: superstitious charms, usually worn around the neck

Short Answer

1. No character, no matter how degraded, is to be despised. Also, we can learn how Newton got so far off track as a young man and how he turned his life around.
2. His father was often gone for long periods and John was left to himself, running about the streets and getting into trouble.
3. Answers will vary.
4. Newton was led into all areas of depravity, and had come to trust in a "wicked system" of living.
5. Because he was now around strangers, he could "appear without disguise," and he used the new situation to sink even lower in depravity and to be as "abandoned as he pleased."
6. He himself was reduced to the condition of a slave. His master's wife treated him with the utmost contempt, even refusing to care for him when he was ill.
7. He thought he could bear the disappointment of his life better in Africa than at home. The thought of marrying a certain young lady finally convinced him.
8. Newton was not a good person. He had mostly wasted all of his potential at this point, and he couldn't see the hand of God as it protected him through this trying period.

Worksheet 43 Answer Key:

Vocabulary

circumspect: careful to consider all circumstances and possible consequences; prudent

tempest: a violent storm

hummocks: rounded knolls or hills

vouchsafe: to grant or furnish, often in a gracious or condescending manner

chimerical: existing only as the product of unchecked imagination; fantastically visionary or improbable

ruminate: to go over in the mind repeatedly and often casually or slowly

mirth: gladness or gaiety as shown by or accompanied with laughter

genteel: of or relating to people who have high social status

Short Answer

1. He found himself calling upon the mercy of the Lord, and then upon further reflection realized that his life was in no way worthy of God's mercy. Thus began a period of deep reflection that eventually led him to restructure the way he was living. There was a serious change wrought in his character.

2. He had become convinced that the gospel of Jesus Christ was indeed true.

3. Answers will vary, but should address the truth of each passage:
   a. He probably saw himself in the parable of the barren fig tree.
   b. He likely identified with the former life of Paul as mentioned in v. 13–14.
   c. His life was much like the prodigal son.

4. Newton nearly lost his life several times at sea and nearly ruined his life by his riotous living. It was only by God's mercy that he survived to become a hero of faith.

5. Newton produced no ill will toward her. It shows that he had indeed been changed into a new man by the grace and mercy of God.

6. At the time, that business was considered "genteel," and because it was a normal practice, few would even consider that it was unjust or sinful. Newton said, "Custom, example, and interest had blinded my eyes."

7. Slavery was still legal in the southern United States. The abolition movement was in its fledgling state in 1831. The author was likely part of that movement (especially considering the statements made about the American Colonization Society).

Worksheet 44 Answer Key:

Vocabulary

diametrically: completely opposed; being at opposite extremes

deplorable: very bad in a way that causes shock, fear, or disgust

Septuagint: a Greek version of the Jewish Scriptures

opulence: wealth, abundance, or influence

conciliating: to make (someone) more friendly or less angry

commiserate: to feel or express sympathy

Short Answer

1. It's a warning to all who exert their influence in corrupting their companions. This old friend was first led astray by Newton. Newton, though now reformed, could not change the mind of this old friend.

2. First, we should consider the miseries that are known in the world. Second, consider all those who we might call "happy." In both cases, we are often better off, though we may not realize it. Answers will vary on part two.

3. Newton was uncharacteristically late for an appointment on a ship. It blew up minutes before his arrival. In another instance, Newton became sick and was unable to go on a voyage that ended up taking the lives of much of the crew.

4. He studied Greek, Hebrew, and Latin so that he could learn the Bible in its original languages.

5. He made them so upon principle, as there might be some men of business in church who had been strangers to his view of the truth, and he did not wish to disgust them, but rather to attract them.

Worksheet 45 Answer Key:

Vocabulary

dogmatical: expressing personal opinions or beliefs as if they are certainly correct and cannot be doubted

unequivocal: very strong and clear; not showing or allowing any doubt

probity: the quality of a person who is completely honest

pillory: a device formerly used for publicly punishing offenders consisting of a wooden frame with holes in which the head and hands can be locked

avocations: activities that you do regularly for enjoyment rather than as a job

impertinent: not restrained within due or proper bounds, especially of propriety or good taste

perspicuous: plain to the understanding, especially because of clarity and precision of presentation

jocular: characterized by jesting; playful

Short Answer

1. Newton argued that some things in Scripture were essential spiritual truths that could have no variance of opinion when interpreted. Other issues, of lesser importance, were not as clear and men should be able to disagree peacefully for the sake of unity in the Body of Christ. Answers will vary on part two.

2. Last words are not nearly as important as all the actions of the years leading up to them.

3. Newton may have been miraculously saved and had his life radically changed, but we should not proceed upon such a hope, because "thousands perish in wrong courses, for one who escapes from their natural consequences."

4. Newton was not a strong speaker and had an ungraceful appearance. He was, however, very gifted at using vibrant illustrations and allusions when preaching. Moreover, it was his tenderness and affection for his congregation that set him apart as an exemplary pastor.

5. He did his best to teach doctrinally accurate sermons.

6. Answers will vary.

Life of Washington — Quiz Answer Keys

Quiz 1 Answer Key:

1. Resolute
2. Huzzahing
3. Approbation
4. Prudent
5. Veneration
6. Sundry
7. Pecuniary
8. Filial
9. Anecdote
10. Unostentatiously
11. Answers will vary, but should focus on a close personal relationship. His mother taught him the importance of truthfulness.
12. Answers will vary, but should address the importance of character and integrity.
13. He was very humble, insisting that he wasn't qualified for such a high post, and refused to be paid for his work.
14. Morale was low. Washington had to take on the role of chief encourager.
15. His men crossed the icy Delaware River on Christmas night and surprise attacked the men on the other side.
16. He had them all inoculated, which had never been done on such a large scale.
17. Answers will vary, but the examples should describe incidents where the protective hand of God was upon Washington and his men.

Quiz 2 Answer Key:

1. Conflagration
2. Fidelity
3. Sloop
4. Dissipation
5. Impious
6. Imprecations
7. Repine
8. Miscreant
9. Wanton
10. Mutiny
11. Washington was willing to eat the same poor provisions as his men — hard bread and a few potatoes. Answers will vary on part two.
12. All three accounts speak of Washington withdrawing privately to engage in prayer.
13. He prayed to his Father in secret, and his Father rewarded him with success against great odds.
14. The order was for soldiers to be punished for excessive swearing — particularly the use of God's name in vain.
15. Arnold wasted much money and as a result tried to give up West Point to the British in return for a high commission in the British Army. His plans were foiled, but he did manage to escape and join the ranks of the British.
16. The man who was watching Washington's home chose to give provisions to the men threatening the fire rather than see the property destroyed. Washington was upset, saying that he'd rather see his home burned than cooperate with the enemy. He said it set a bad example. Answers will vary on part two.
17. Answers will vary, but the examples should describe incidents where the protective hand of God was upon Washington and his men.

Quiz 3 Answer Key:

1. Homage
2. Rectitude
3. Insolent
4. Privateer
5. Eminence
6. Concourse
7. Felicity
8. Diffidence
9. Tranquility
10. Deportment
11. He told them not to celebrate, but rather to let all of history celebrate for them.
12. He sent fifteen hundred men to quell these mutineers, and contrasted their deplorable behavior to the veterans who had endured nakedness, hunger, and cold.
13. You should enjoy the great blessing of freedom from unjust and oppressive laws, but you should beware of resisting the righteous laws of God. Freedom is not a license to sin, but an opportunity to worship the Creator.
14. He was hesitant to serve, arguing that he lacked the political skills necessary. He humbly submitted to the will of the people promising only "integrity and firmness."
15. There was war between France and England. Washington wanted the United States to stay neutral. He knew that the nation couldn't afford to be drawn into another war.
16. Congress had passed a tax on whiskey, and a number of backwoods farmers were committing violent acts in protest. Washington quickly organized a large group of troops to be sent out and quell the rebellion. They did so without bloodshed.
17. Answers will vary, but should discuss the mutual respect between the two.

Quiz 4 Answer Key:

1. Dispositions
2. Trifling
3. Benefactor
4. Inculcated
5. Indigent
6. Solicitude

7. Proffered
8. Abhorrence
9. Idleness
10. Frank
11. Religion and morality are "indispensable supports" for political prosperity.
12. Answers could include (but aren't limited to): He paid for education for the poor, he kept a portion of his wheat to give to the needy, and he even let an old attendant of General Braddock live on his farm for the rest of his life.
13. The French had failed to negotiate in good faith with American envoys sent there to preserve peace. Our nation neared war with the French.
14. Washington went out into the cold to review his farm. He developed a severe cold. The doctors tried various primitive treatments including bleeding at least three times. He finally succumbed on December 14, 1799.
15. Answers will vary. There is much evidence to the contrary. A great deal of Washington's public statements show a clear respect for God and view Him as an active force in the world. The conclusion includes the testimony of household servants and relatives who observed Washington's private prayer and devotional life.
16. Answers will vary, but should include specific reasons as to why Washington is worthy of our imitation. Topics that could be addressed include his wisdom, leadership, honesty, control of passions, universal respect, strong faith in God, etc.

Life of Andrew Jackson — Quiz Answer Keys

Quiz 5 Answer Key:

1. affability
2. morose
3. censure
4. torpor
5. habiliments
6. incipient
7. churlishness
8. assuage
9. provocation
10. privations
11. Many people loved Jackson and many others hated him. But whatever the case, you couldn't ignore him. He was a bold person who provoked bold feelings.
12. Jackson was taken prisoner by the British. He refused to clean a soldier's boots, stating that he should be treated with the respect a prisoner of war is due. The soldier struck at the young Jackson's head with his sword, but the blow was deflected by Jackson's left hand.
13. He was exposed to many dangers, but never seemed to flinch. He developed strong leadership skills, often leading groups of people through this untamed wilderness. He also developed a reputation for being someone who shouldn't be provoked to anger.
14. There was a dispute between the two over a horse-racing incident. Insults and letters were exchanged over a period of days until Jackson challenged him to duel on May 23. This incident reveals several insights into the nature of Andrew Jackson: he was fiercely loyal, he was chivalrous to a fault, he had no fear of anyone or death itself, and he was given to hotheadedness.
15. Jackson promptly sold his plantation, paid his debts, and moved into a log cabin. He quickly was able to recover, however. Answers will vary on part two.
16. Answers will vary, but should focus on Jackson's personal characteristics.
17. Answers should include, but aren't limited to: Washington and Jackson both developed a reputation as fearless in battle, natural leaders, American patriots, and men who inspired the love and devotion of their troops. Jackson, however, had also developed the reputation of being hotheaded, temperamental, angry, and violent. Whereas Washington learned to harness his anger, it seems that Jackson had not.

Quiz 6 Answer Key:

1. lassitude
2. trepidation
3. prevaricate
4. intrepidity
5. accoutrements
6. amicable
7. satiety
8. auspiciously
9. ardor
10. chagrined
11. Jackson adopted him and raised him as his own son. Some say this incident proves that Jackson wasn't just a heartless killer of Indians; others say it was done just to soften his image. In either case, it surely proves that Jackson was a complex person. This complexity is largely why historians are so divided on his merits.
12. He played the volunteers against the militia; he pleaded with the men; he bought time with the little provisions he was able to acquire; and ultimately he threatened to kill them all or die trying.
13. Answers can vary greatly on this set of questions.
14. Like Washington, Jackson also provided for others without the recipient knowing the source.
15. Jackson sent him to his own house in Tennessee and got him started in business when the war ended.
16. Answers will vary, but must give evidence in support.
17. "He is a man who intends when he gives an order that it shall be obeyed," replied Gordon. Milton decided that he would, on second thought, give the assistance that Jackson requested. Answers will vary on part two, but should be sure to show the complexity of his character.

Quiz 7 Answer Key:

1. impervious
2. alacrity
3. nefarious
4. assiduity
5. judicious
6. conjecture
7. incessant
8. glacis
9. galled
10. licentious
11. Martial law is the law administered by military forces that is invoked by a government in an emergency when the civilian law enforcement agencies are unable to maintain public order and safety. Jackson put New Orleans under martial law because he believed that there were too many subversive individuals in the city to keep it safe during the course of anticipated attack. Most of the settlers there were Spanish or French and may not have had too much patriotism toward the United States.
12. Jackson believed that since the British had vastly superior numbers, that another attack in daylight could prove fatal to the Americans. Moreover, he found it more important that the city of New Orleans be protected and not fall into the hands of the opposition.
13. Clear-headed sagacity, promptness of decision, and rapidity of execution
14. Good men are a greater guarantee for success than any fortification one could build with hands.
15. Answers will vary, but should focus on the example that Jackson set.
16. He was implying that Jackson set a personal example of diligence and his constant presence imbued the men with confidence.
17. The most significant factor was that Jackson had carefully selected the battlefield and built entrenchments that were very difficult to assault. He, of course, gave the credit to the valiant men who served under his command. He was also careful to keep treason from undermining his efforts, and made strategic decisions to not pursue and conquer when the odds were not in his favor.

Quiz 8 Answer Key:

1. rapine
2. temerity
3. encomium
4. plenipotentiary
5. averred
6. parlance
7. incendiaries
8. celerity
9. asperity
10. writ of habeas corpus
11. Jackson supporters filled the streets and quickly raised the fine to pay on his behalf. Jackson refused the money and paid the fine himself. The money raised for his support was given to a charitable institution at his request.
12. This text indicates that it is an allusion to his successful raids in the sacred Indian "Hickory Ground."
13. Answers will vary, but hopefully will acknowledge that while being a good trait, a leader ought to still be able to vary his or her opinion once proven wrong.
14. Jackson received more electoral votes than any of the other candidates, but the House of Representatives chose John Quincy Adams instead. Speaker of the House Henry Clay was then chosen to be Secretary of State for Adams. Many believe that this arrangement was made in order to get the House to pick Adams over Jackson.
15. In typical Jackson fashion, he stated that if he had known the man's intentions when he came in the room, he could assure you "that he would never again have the temerity to undertake such a thing."
16. "In the hands of a merciful God, I have full confidence. . . . I am ready to depart when called. The Bible is true. . . . Upon that sacred volume I rest my hope of eternal salvation, through the merits and blood of our blessed Lord and Savior, Jesus Christ."
17. He was prompt and resolute in battle; his courage and fortitude were unmatched; his readiness to adapt and succeed in any situation; he never forgot a favor or failed to remember a friend.

Life of Luther — Quiz Answer Keys

Quiz 9 Answer Key:

1. turbid
2. mendicant
3. vitiated
4. genuflection
5. cogitations
6. declivity
7. capacious
8. demure
9. pensive
10. penury
11. It is a rather scathing critique: "a religion of law rather than of gospel; a Pelagian system of works rather than of divine grace . . . a religion of the senses and of a poetical imagination rather than of saving faith . . . a religion founded more on the ignorance and superstition of the middle ages than on the revelation of the truth by Jesus Christ and His apostles." (See page 35.)
12. She was pious, but much more religiously superstitious than his father. Her influence is one of the greatest reasons Luther chose to become a monk in the first place.
13. Luther stumbled across a Bible while looking through other books. He marveled because the Bible contained much more than the postils circulated in the churches. He quickly devoured the story of Hannah and Samuel, and he began to wish for the day that he would one day have a Bible of his own. Answers will vary, but the Word of God was kept from the masses of people.

14. Justification by faith alone, and private judgment in interpreting Scripture

15. In his view, this pious life would be the surest way of pleasing God. He was nearly struck by lightning, and in his terror made this rash vow.

16. The Bible was not studied as a whole, but in small pieces removed from context. The author could not be his own interpreter. The literal sense was "deserted at pleasure, and an allegorical one introduced to suit the object of the interpreter."

17. He was able to connect well with the greatest mass of people. His homely manner of speaking and writing served him with a great advantage. In addition, he came from a part of Germany that was "the most German" of all the districts, and it belonged to no other section. The Reformation also coincided with a larger period of social unrest among the peasantry.

Quiz 10 Answer Key:

1. ablution
2. cumbrous
3. decorous
4. ignominiously
5. obstreperous
6. mien
7. lucre
8. erudite
9. exculpate
10. pernicious
11. Staupitz actually encouraged Luther to study the Scripture. He also nurtured many of the spiritual questions Luther was beginning to have. He was one of the primary instigators of Luther's conversion to evangelicalism.
12. A priest was to be a mediator between God and man. Luther was so conscious of his sinfulness that he was terrified to hold such an exalted position.
13. Catholic: God is foremost a judge to be feared; good works are sought as a recommendation to God. Protestant: God is a loving Savior who forgives gratuitously, meeting the sinner where he is and bearing his load.

14. The only Bible he had at his disposal was the Latin Vulgate, which in his estimation was full of errors. Being able to read the Bible in the original languages would provide a significant advantage to overcoming these errors.

15. Luther had taken an oath to teach purely and sincerely to the Scriptures. Catholic leaders supposed there was a substantial agreement between the teachings of the church and those of the Bible. Once Luther came under the conviction that the church's teachings were not biblical, he then used the oath he had taken as justification for his agitation.

16. He said, "When I go up into the pulpit, I do not look upon any one. I think them to be only so many blocks before me, and I speak out the words of my God." Answers will vary on part two.

17. Answers will vary, but a summary should include basic ideas such as these — Social: he had reluctantly taken positions of leadership, but that reluctance began to fall away, and a newfound boldness is seen in his letters. Intellectual: he had begun to attack much of the philosophical teachings in the university and the church. Theological: he had fully adopted the concept of salvation by faith alone, and began to openly attack the idea of a works-based faith.

Quiz 11 Answer Key:

1. fulminate
2. odium
3. corpulent
4. servile
5. plenary
6. transient
7. promulgated
8. puerile
9. supercilious
10. magnanimity
11. In effect, indulgences had become a tax for sins.
12. Contrition, confession, and satisfaction.

Luther had three major questions: How was one to know that his penitence was sufficient? How would he be sure that no individual sin was omitted in the confession? Why should absolution be pronounced before the conditions were all fulfilled, before satisfaction was known to be made?

13. The 95 theses were not written for an audience of laymen. They were "ill adapted for the common people." But once they had been taken and published by his friends, he found it necessary to write a more colloquial version for the general public.

14. He would rather people give their money to the poor, because there was a clear biblical basis for it, while the biblical basis for indulgences was questionable in his eyes. Moreover, he saw grace as a free gift of God, making indulgences unnecessary. He refused to administer the supper, unless they first made confession. This was because he felt that repentance was being overlooked in this whole process, and without repentance, none of the other religious trappings really mattered.

15. Answers will vary, but the evidence shows that even into late 1518, although he was subversive to the Church leaders, he was still willing to submit to their questions . . . if they would ever offer them.

16. Answers will vary.

17. Answers will vary, but should have specific examples of weaknesses.

Quiz 12 Answer Key:

1. aspersion
2. jocosely
3. sycophancy
4. garrulity
5. perfidious
6. gesticulation
7. spurious
8. disingenuous
9. escutcheon
10. iota
11. It was useful for the cause of the Reformation in opening the eyes of Luther himself on the whole subject of papal authority, and in drawing public attention to the issue. It caused a few papists to join him, but it created an even greater opposition to his teachings among the others. Many of Luther's troubles that came in the next year or two were a direct result of this debate (page 294).
12. Luther's commentary on the Epistle to the Galatians
13. Luther fully expected to lose his life, much like Huss had. This shows the courage and resolve that Luther possessed, and it shows how deeply he believed in his theological findings.
14. Answers will vary, but will likely focus on Luther's bravery, resolve, and eloquence in defending the faith.
15. People everywhere began to exercise freedom of opinion and speech. Schisms developed over several questions: How is this freedom to be controlled? Shall men be free to differ from Luther himself? Is there no subjection to authority in matters of religion? Shall the civil power be brought in as the protector of true faith?
16. Carlstadt insisted on bringing back the pattern of the primitive church in its entirety. He opposed all ceremonies introduced by the later church. Luther was somewhat indifferent on matters of outward conformity, preferring to focus on inward manifestations of faith.
17. They piled up his books on a table and asked, "Are these your books, and will you retract them or their contents?" Luther admitted the books were his, but asked for more time to contemplate the second question. They gave him until the next day to answer. The following day, he argued that his books were of three different classes. Some were clearly and simply harmless, and he couldn't renounce those. Some were directed against the pope and Rome, and if he were to revoke these, he would give strength to tyranny. The third class was directed against individuals. He admitted these to be too harsh in tone, but

he would not be able to revoke these either. He closed with this: "Unless I shall be convinced by the testimony of Scripture, or by clear and plain argument . . . I am held by those passages which I have cited, and am bound by my conscience and by the word of God, and therefore I may not — cannot retract, inasmuch as it is neither safe nor right to violate my conscience. Here I stand, and cannot do otherwise, God be my help. Amen."

Quiz 13 Answer Key:

1. avarice
2. ribaldry
3. fetters
4. dissimulation
5. expostulation
6. inveterate
7. harangued
8. pertinacity
9. castigate
10. circumlocution
11. Answers will vary, but should clearly attempt to explain the source of this character flaw, and the potential change a different attitude could have had on his efforts.
12. Luther was very concerned about the Reformation being discredited by the mass political movements that sometimes resulted in fanaticism. As a result, he held to divine right of kings and the doctrine of passive obedience on the part of their subjects. He traveled about trying to quell the democratic fervor sweeping the masses.
13. He was a poor manager of money. He was accustomed to living on very little from his days as a monk, and he was extraordinarily generous to the needy, so much so that he often found himself in debt. His wife was a much shrewder manager of funds.
14. He figured his life to always be in jeopardy and hated to enter into matrimony only to leave behind a grieving wife.
15. He was experienced — he preached every day and often multiple times. He preached in the native language, which was compelling for this time. His appearance helped — his manly form, his piercing eyes, and his penetrating voice. His intelligence, wit, quickness of memory, and his poetic composition should be considered. Most importantly, he preached the gospel, and people were moved by its message and the conviction with which Luther communicated it.
16. If people were going to be their own interpreter of Scripture, they needed a solid education to undergird their studies. He believed that parents had a biblical responsibility to educate their children.
17. Answers will vary. Some positive qualities would include his brilliant mind, unswerving devotion, fearlessness, etc. Some negative qualities would include his combativeness, his tendency toward dispute and pettiness, his abrasive language, his frequent fits of melancholy, etc.

Life of John Knox Quiz Answer Keys

Quiz 14 Answer Key:

1. effrontery
2. thralldom
3. indurate
4. retinue
5. indefatigable
6. artifice
7. actuated
8. dauphin
9. languid
10. apoplectic
11. His burning zeal and unbending faithfulness
12. Properly qualified persons should be able to read the Scriptures every Lord's day; the sacraments should be administered in the language of the people; preaching and the interpretation of Scripture should be private.

13. The talents which are suited to one age and station would be altogether unsuitable to another, and we should keep in mind that what is needed for the furtherance of God's kingdom will be different from age to age.
14. Like Luther, Knox was also very hesitant to teach. Both felt a great weight of responsibility in holding such a high office.
15. There was much distrust between the two. She was queen, yet she feared Knox because of his popularity among a vast number in her country. Knox was emboldened by God, but also knew that Mary couldn't touch him without arousing serious consequences.
16. He says that these characteristics were "absolutely necessary" for constituting a reformer. If he had been gentler in spirit, he would have been unfit for the task that God had called him to. Answers will vary on part two.
17. Answers will vary, but should focus on the boldness and outspoken manner which both men displayed throughout their lives.

Life of John Newton — Quiz Answer Keys

Quiz 15 Answer Key:

1. caprices
2. probity
3. commiserate
4. mirth
5. perspicuous
6. Newton nearly lost his life several times at sea, and nearly ruined his life by his riotous living. It was only by God's mercy that he survived to become a hero of faith.
7. Newton was not a strong speaker and had an ungraceful appearance. He was, however, very gifted at using vibrant illustrations and allusions when preaching. Moreover, it was his tenderness and affection for his congregation that set him apart as an exemplary pastor.
8. Answers will vary, but should include a description of two incidents. Newton nearly lost his life several times at sea, and nearly ruined his life by his riotous living.
9. The biographical sketch should include the details of Newton's depraved life before Christ, and the miraculous change thereafter. Answers will vary on part two, but should at least include a discussion of the power of God to change the worst of sinners. (The student may need extra time to complete this question.)

Christian Bios — Test Answer Keys

Test 1 (Washington) Answer Key:

1. Trifling
2. Eminence
3. Pecuniary
4. Approbation
5. Repine
6. Imprecations
7. Diffidence
8. Conflagration
9. Veneration
10. Frank
11. Answers will vary, but the examples should describe incidents where the protective hand of God was upon Washington and his men.
12. Answers should focus on his faith in God, wisdom, restraint, care for the poor, etc. Make sure specific information is given.
13. Answers will vary, but should include specific reasons as to why Washington is worthy of our imitation. Topics that could be addressed include his wisdom, leadership, honesty, control of passions, universal respect, strong faith in God, etc.
14. Answers will vary. There is much evidence to the contrary. A great deal of Washington's public statements show a clear respect for God and view Him as an active force in the world. The conclusion includes the testimony of household servants and relatives who observed Washington's private prayer and devotional life.

Test 2 (Andrew Jackson) Answer Key:

1. censure
2. habiliments
3. privations
4. amicable
5. prevaricate
6. assiduity
7. alacrity
8. plenipotentiary
9. parlance
10. rapine
11. Jackson was a complex man. He battled his enemies with relentless ferocity, yet he adopted an Indian boy and raised him as his own. He was stern, stubborn, and unmovable once his mind was made up. He was harsh on those who opposed him, yet kind, compassionate, and gentle to those he loved. He was born into harsh circumstance, yet still managed to ascend to the highest office in the land. His confidence and personality seeped into everything he touched. Love him or hate him, but you can't ignore that he was an exceptional American.
12. The most significant factor was that Jackson had carefully selected the battlefield and built entrenchments that were very difficult to assault. He, of course, gave the credit to the valiant men who served under his command. He was also careful to keep treason from undermining his efforts, and made strategic decisions to not pursue and conquer when the odds were not in his favor.
13. He was prompt and resolute in battle; his courage and fortitude were unmatched; his readiness to adapt and succeed in any situation; he never forgot a favor or failed to remember a friend (among many other things).
14. Answers will vary, but should provide multiple examples given in the texts.

Test 3 (Luther) Answer Key:

1. capacious
2. fulminate
3. ignominiously
4. plenary
5. erudite
6. ribaldry
7. garrulity
8. perfidious

9. penury
10. pernicious
11. Catholic: God is foremost a judge to be feared; good works are sought as a recommendation to God. Protestant: God is a loving Savior who forgives gratuitously, meeting the sinner where he is and bearing his load. Moreover, Luther fiercely defended the right of the individual to be his own interpreter of Scripture.
12. He was able to connect well with the greatest mass of people. His homely manner of speaking and writing served him with a great advantage. In addition, he came from a part of Germany that was "the most German" of all the districts, and it belonged to no other section. The Reformation also coincided with a larger period of social unrest among the peasantry.
13. They piled up his books on a table and asked, "Are these your books, and will you retract them or their contents?" Luther admitted the books were his, but asked for more time to contemplate the second question. They gave him until the next day to answer. The following day, he argued that his books were of three different classes. Some were clearly and simply harmless, and he couldn't renounce those. Some were directed against the pope and Rome, and if he were to revoke these, he would give strength to tyranny. The third class was directed against individuals. He admitted these to be too harsh in tone, but he would not be able to revoke these either. He closed with this: "Unless I shall be convinced by the testimony of Scripture, or by clear and plain argument . . . I am held by those passages which I have cited, and am bound by my conscience and by the word of God, and therefore I may not — cannot retract, inasmuch as it is neither safe nor right to violate my conscience. Here I stand, and cannot do otherwise, God be my help. Amen."
14. Answers will vary. Some positive qualities would include his brilliant mind, unswerving devotion, fearlessness, etc. Some negative qualities would include his combativeness, his tendency toward dispute and pettiness, his abrasive language, his frequent fits of melancholy, etc.

Test 4 (Knox and Newton) Answer Key:

1. caprices
2. indefatigable
3. thralldom
4. effrontery
5. mirth
6. commiserate
7. indurate
8. retinue
9. probity
10. languid
11. He says that these characteristics were "absolutely necessary" for constituting a reformer. If he had been gentler in spirit, he would have been unfit for the task that God had called him to. Answers will vary on part two.
12. Answers will vary, but should focus on the boldness and outspoken manner which both men displayed throughout their lives.
13. Answers will vary, but should include a description of two incidents. Newton nearly lost his life several times at sea, and nearly ruined his life by his riotous living.
14. The biographical sketch should include the details of Newton's depraved life before Christ, and the miraculous change thereafter. Answers will vary on part two, but should at least include a discussion of the power of God to change the worst of sinners.

Parent Lesson Plan — Promotion

Now turn your favorite **Master Books** into curriculum! Each Parent Lesson Plan (PLP) includes:

- An easy-to-follow, one-year educational calendar
- Helpful worksheets, quizzes, tests, and answer keys
- Additional teaching helps and insights
- Complete with all you need to quickly and easily begin your education program today!

ELEMENTARY ZOOLOGY

1 year
4th – 6th

Package Includes: *World of Animals; Dinosaur Activity Book; The Complete Aquarium Adventure; The Complete Zoo Adventure; Parent Lesson Planner*

5 Book Package
978-0-89051-747-5 $84.99

SCIENCE STARTERS: ELEMENTARY PHYSICAL & EARTH SCIENCE

1 year
3rd – 6th grade

6 Book Package Includes: *Forces & Motion –Student, Student Journal, and Teacher; The Earth – Student, Teacher & Student Journal; Parent Lesson Planner*

6 Book Package
978-0-89051-748-2 $51.99

SCIENCE STARTERS: ELEMENTARY CHEMISTRY & PHYSICS

1 year
3rd – 6th grade

Package Includes: *Matter – Student, Student Journal, and Teacher; Energy – Student, Teacher, & Student Journal; Parent Lesson Planner*

7 Book Package
978-0-89051-749-9 $54.99

INTRO TO METEOROLOGY & ASTRONOMY

1 year
7th – 9th grade
½ Credit

Package Includes: *The Weather Book; The New Astronomy Book; Parent Lesson Planner*

3 Book Package
978-0-89051-753-6 $45.99

INTRO TO OCEANOGRAPHY & ECOLOGY

1 year
7th – 9th grade
½ Credit

Package Includes: *The Ocean Book; The Ecology Book; Parent Lesson Planner*

3 Book Package
978-0-89051-754-3 $45.99

INTRO TO SPELEOLOGY & PALEONTOLOGY

1 year
7th – 9th grade
½ Credit

Package Includes: *The Cave Book; The Fossil Book; Parent Lesson Planner*

3 Book Package
978-0-89051-752-9 $44.99

CONCEPTS OF MEDICINE & BIOLOGY

1 year
7th – 9th grade
½ Credit

Package Includes: *Exploring the History of Medicine; Exploring the World of Biology; Parent Lesson Planner*

3 Book Package
978-0-89051-756-7 $40.99

CONCEPTS OF MATHEMATICS & PHYSICS

1 year
7th – 9th grade
½ Credit

Package Includes: *Exploring the World of Mathematics; Exploring the World of Physics; Parent Lesson Planner*

3 Book Package
978-0-89051-757-4 $40.99

CONCEPTS OF EARTH SCIENCE & CHEMISTRY

1 year
7th – 9th grade
½ Credit

Package Includes: *Exploring Planet Earth; Exploring the World of Chemistry; Parent Lesson Planner*

3 Book Package
978-0-89051-755-0 $40.99

THE SCIENCE OF LIFE: BIOLOGY

1 year
8th – 9th grade
½ Credit

Package Includes: *Building Blocks in Science; Building Blocks in Life Science; Parent Lesson Planner*

3 Book Package
978-0-89051-758-1 $44.99

BASIC PRE-MED

1 year
8th – 9th grade
½ Credit

Package Includes: *The Genesis of Germs; The Building Blocks in Life Science; Parent Lesson Planner*

3 Book Package
978-0-89051-759-8 $43.99

Parent Lesson Plan — Promotion

INTRO TO ASTRONOMY

1 year
7th – 9th grade
½ Credit

Package Includes: *The Stargazer's Guide to the Night Sky; Parent Lesson Planner*

2 Book Package
978-0-89051-760-4 $47.99

INTRO TO ARCHAEOLOGY & GEOLOGY

1 year
7th – 9th
½ Credit

Package Includes: *The Archaeology Book; The Geology Book; Parent Lesson Planner*

3 Book Package
978-0-89051-751-2 $45.99

SURVEY OF SCIENCE HISTORY & CONCEPTS

1 year
10th – 12th grade
1 Credit

Package Includes: *The World of Mathematics; The World of Physics; The World of Biology; The World of Chemistry; Parent Lesson Planner*

5 Book Package
978-0-89051-764-2 $72.99

SURVEY OF SCIENCE SPECIALTIES

1 year
10th – 12th grade
1 Credit

Package Includes: *The Cave Book; The Fossil Book; The Geology Book; The Archaeology Book; Parent Lesson Planner*

5 Book Package
978-0-89051-765-9 $81.99

SURVEY OF ASTRONOMY

1 year
10th – 12th grade
1 Credit

Package Includes: *The Stargazers Guide to the Night Sky; Our Created Moon; Taking Back Astronomy; Our Created Moon DVD; Created Cosmos DVD; Parent Lesson Planner*

4 Book, 2 DVD Package
978-0-89051-766-6 $113.99

GEOLOGY & BIBLICAL HISTORY

1 year
8th – 9th
1 Credit

Package Includes: *Explore the Grand Canyon; Explore Yellowstone; Explore Yosemite & Zion National Parks; Your Guide to the Grand Canyon; Your Guide to Yellowstone; Your Guide to Zion & Bryce Canyon National Parks; Parent Lesson Planner.*

4 Book, 3 DVD Package
978-0-89051-750-5 $108.99

PALEONTOLOGY: LIVING FOSSILS

1 year
10th – 12th grade
½ Credit

Package Includes: *Living Fossils, Living Fossils Teacher Guide, Living Fossils DVD; Parent Lesson Planner*

3 Book, 1 DVD Package
978-0-89051-763-5 $66.99

LIFE SCIENCE ORIGINS & SCIENTIFIC THEORY

1 year
10th – 12th grade
1 Credit

Package Includes: *Evolution: the Grand Experiment, Teacher Guide, DVD; Living Fossils, Teacher Guide, DVD; Parent Lesson Planner*

5 Book, 2 DVD Package
978-0-89051-761-1 $144.99

NATURAL SCIENCE THE STORY OF ORIGINS

1 year
10th – 12th grade
½ Credit

Package Includes: *Evolution: the Grand Experiment; Evolution: the Grand Experiment Teacher's Guide, Evolution: the Grand Experiment DVD; Parent Lesson Planner*

3 Book, 1 DVD Package
978-0-89051-762-8 $71.99

ADVANCED PRE-MED STUDIES

1 year
10th – 12th grade
1 Credit

Package Includes: *Building Blocks in Life Science; The Genesis of Germs; Body by Design; Exploring the History of Medicine; Parent Lesson Planner*

5 Book Package
978-0-89051-767-3 $76.99

BIBLICAL ARCHAEOLOGY

1 year
10th – 12th grade
1 Credit

Package Includes: *Unwrapping the Pharaohs; Unveiling the Kings of Israel; The Archaeology Book; Parent Lesson Planner.*

4 Book Package
978-0-89051-768-0 $99.99

CHRISTIAN HERITAGE

1 year
10th – 12th grade
1 Credit

Package Includes: *For You They Signed; Lesson Parent Planner*

2 Book Package
978-0-89051-769-7 $50.99

masterbooks.net

SCIENCE STARTERS: ELEMENTARY GENERAL SCIENCE & ASTRONOMY

1 year
3rd – 6th grade

Package Includes: *Water & Weather – Student, Student Journal, and Teacher; The Universe – Student, Teacher, & Student Journal; Parent Lesson Planner*

7 Book Package
978-0-89051-816-8 $54.99

APPLIED SCIENCE: STUDIES OF GOD'S DESIGN IN NATURE

1 year
7th – 9th grade
1 Credit

Package Includes: *Made in Heaven, Champions of Invention, Discovery of Design, & Parent Lesson Planner*

4 Book Package
978-0-89051-812-0 $50.99

ELEMENTARY WORLD HISTORY

1 year
3rd – 6th

Package Includes: *The Big Book of History; Noah's Ark: Thinking Outside the Box (book and DVD); & Parent Lesson Planner*

3 Book, 1 DVD Package
978-0-89051-815-1 $66.96

CONCEPTS OF BIOGEOLOGY & ASTRONOMY

1 year
7th – 9th grade
½ Credit

Package Includes: *Exploring the World Around You, Exploring the World of Astronomy, & Parent Lesson Planner*

3 Book Package
978-0-89051-813-7 $41.99

ELEMENTARY GEOGRAPHY AND CULTURES

1 year
3rd – 6th grade

Package Includes: *Children's Atlas of God's World, Passport to the World, & Parent Lesson Planner*

3 Book Package
978-0-89051-814-4 $49.99

INTRO TO BIBLICAL GREEK

½ year language studies
10th – 12th
½ Credit

Package Includes: *It's Not Greek to Me DVD & Parent Lesson Planner*

1 Book, 1 DVD Package
978-0-89051-818-2 $33.99

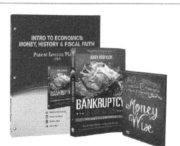

INTRO TO ECONOMICS: MONEY, HISTORY, & FISCAL FAITH

½ year economics
10th – 12th
½ Credit

Package Includes: *Bankruptcy of Our Nation, Money Wise DVD, & Parent Lesson Planner*

2 Book, 4 DVD Package
978-0-89051-811-3 $57.99

Master Books®

P.O. Box 726
Green Forest, AR 72638

Visit masterbooks.net for additional information, look insides, video trailers, and more!